Human–Computer Interaction Series

Human-Computer Interaction

Panos Markopoulos [iD]
Eindhoven University of Technology, Eindhoven, The Netherlands

Brad A. Myers
Carnegie Mellon University, Pittsburgh, USA

Philippe Palanque [iD]
University of Toulouse, Toulouse, France

Albrecht Schmidt
Universität Stuttgart, Stuttgart, Germany

Holger Schnädelbach [iD]
Holger Schnädelbach Adaptive Architecture—HSAA, Berlin, Germany

Ahmed Seffah
Concordia University, Montreal, Finland

Radu-Daniel Vatavu
University Stefan cel Mare Suceava, Suceava, Romania

Frank Vetere
University of Melbourne, Melbourne, Australia

Shengdong Zhao
National University of Singapore, Singapore, Singapore

Vladimir Geroimenko

Communication Skills for Generative AI

The Essential Guide for Humans

Vladimir Geroimenko
The British University in Egypt
Cairo, Egypt

ISSN 1571-5035   ISSN 2524-4477 (electronic)
Human–Computer Interaction Series
ISSN 2520-1670   ISSN 2520-1689 (electronic)
SpringerBriefs in Human-Computer Interaction
ISBN 978-3-032-21688-5   ISBN 978-3-032-21689-2 (eBook)
https://doi.org/10.1007/978-3-032-21689-2

This Springer imprint is published by the registered company Springer Nature Switzerland AG
The registered company address is: Gewerbestrasse 11, 6330 Cham, Switzerland

If disposing of this product, please recycle the paper.

To the British University in Egypt and to its Chair of the Board of Trustees, Ms. Farida Khamis.

Preface

This book is the final volume in a trilogy devoted to understanding how humans communicate with generative artificial intelligence. The trilogy consists of:

- *The Essential Guide to Prompt Engineering: Key Principles, Techniques, Challenges, and Security Risks* (Springer, 2025)
- *Beyond and After Prompt Engineering: The Future of AI Communication* (Springer, 2026)
- *Communication Skills for Generative AI: The Essential Guide for Humans* (Springer, 2026).

Together, these works trace a rapid conceptual transition: from prompt engineering as a technical practice toward AI communication as a broader human competence. While the first book established foundational principles and techniques, and the second explored emerging and future-facing paradigms, the present volume consolidates these insights into a coherent framework of communication skills that humans increasingly need in everyday, professional and academic interaction with generative AI.

This book argues that effective interaction with generative AI is no longer primarily a matter of crafting better prompts. Instead, it is a matter of developing communicative awareness: understanding how AI systems interpret intent, context, constraints, tone and dialogue over time. As generative models become more capable, more multimodal and more deeply integrated into human workflows, the quality of outcomes depends less on isolated instructions and more on sustained, reflective communication.

The book is intentionally conceptual rather than procedural. It does not offer prompt templates or technical shortcuts. Instead, it presents communication principles, techniques and reflective practices that remain applicable across tools, models and future system architectures. To support clarity and conceptual grounding, the book is richly illustrated with 42 original conceptual diagrams, each accompanied by detailed explanatory captions.

Given the subject matter, it is important to be transparent about how this book was created. Like my previous works, this volume was written through a deliberate process of human–AI collaboration. Generative AI systems were not merely objects of analysis but active participants in the drafting and refinement process. The goal was not automation, but augmentation: combining human conceptual judgement with AI's generative and analytical capacities.

The writing process followed a structured methodology. It began with conceptualisation and research into human–AI communication, drawing on academic literature, emerging practices and speculative perspectives. Drafting was then supported by multiple leading AI models, including ChatGPT, Claude and Gemini, each prompted from different conceptual angles to surface diverse viewpoints. Their outputs were analysed, synthesised and critically evaluated against my own research notes. Extensive iterative editing ensured coherence, conceptual consistency, and factual accuracy, with full human oversight at every stage. Final quality checks focused on clarity, originality and tone, followed by careful manual proofreading.

In this sense, the book is itself a practical demonstration of its central thesis. We did not merely write about human–AI communication; we practised it. The progression from principles to techniques, from pitfalls to collaboration and from metacommunication to reflective closure unfolded through iterative alignment, negotiated intent and shared reasoning. Human responsibility remained central throughout.

This experience reinforces a key claim of the book: meaningful human–AI collaboration is already possible with today's tools, provided that humans develop the communicative skills to guide, evaluate, and reflect on AI behaviour. At the same time, it foreshadows a future in which communication with AI becomes more fluid, more relational and more deeply embedded in human cognition and creativity.

If this book succeeds, it will help readers move beyond viewing AI as a system to be controlled and towards engaging it as a communicative partner—one that requires clarity, reflection and responsibility in equal measure.

Cairo, Egypt   Vladimir Geroimenko
May 2026

Competing Interests The author has no competing interests to declare that are relevant to the content of this manuscript.

Contents

About the Author

Dr. Vladimir Geroimenko is a professor at the Faculty of Informatics and Computer Science at the British University in Egypt, Cairo. He is an internationally recognised scholar whose research spans human–AI communication, prompt engineering, cognitive science, augmented reality and emerging digital technologies.

Dr. Geroimenko has authored and edited 24 books, 17 of which have been published by Springer. His recent research monographs include *Beyond and After Prompt Engineering: The Future of AI Communication* (Springer, 2026), *The Essential Guide to Prompt Engineering: Key Principles, Techniques, Challenges, and Security Risks* (Springer, 2025), *Augmented Reality and Artificial Intelligence: The Fusion of Advanced Technologies* (Springer, 2023) and *Augmented Reality Art: From an Emerging Technology to a Novel Creative Medium* (3rd ed., Springer, 2022).

He received his M.Sc. degree in Physics and Mathematics from Vitebsk State University (Belarus) in 1976, followed by a Ph.D. in the Methodology of Science from the Belarusian Academy of Sciences in Minsk in 1982. In 1990, he was awarded a higher Doctor of Science (D.Sc.) degree in Cognitive Sciences from Belarusian State University. From 1982 to 1998, he worked at the Belarusian Academy of Sciences, where he conducted research in the methodology of science and human–computer cognitive models.

Dr. Geroimenko has held several international research and academic appointments, including Research Fellow of the Alexander von Humboldt Foundation at Ruhr University Bochum, Germany (1991–1993), and Visiting Professor at the SSKKII Centre for Cognitive Science at the University of Gothenburg, Sweden (1995–1998). In 1998, he joined the University of Plymouth, UK, as a Reader in Multimedia and Web Technology. Since September 2016, he has been a professor of Informatics and Computer Science at the British University in Egypt.

Chapter 1
Introduction: Why Humans Need AI Communication Skills

The rise of generative AI has created an unprecedented form of interaction in which humans communicate with systems capable of producing language, interpreting context and supporting reasoning. This development challenges traditional models of human–computer interaction and introduces the need for new communicative competencies that extend beyond technical prompting. As generative AI becomes integrated into daily life and professional practice, understanding how to express intentions clearly, negotiate meaning and collaborate effectively with intelligent systems becomes essential. This chapter provides a conceptual foundation for these emerging skills.

1.1 From Prompt Engineering to Comprehensive AI Communication

When the first generation of large-scale generative AI systems became widely accessible in 2022, users quickly discovered that the quality of the output depended almost entirely on the quality of their input. This emergent skill—soon called *prompt engineering*—appeared to offer a reliable method for extracting useful, accurate and creative results from models whose internal operations were largely opaque. Early adopters experimented with templates, keywords, system prompts and highly structured formulations designed to 'force' the model into a particular role or style. Within months, prompt engineering was enthusiastically embraced across technical, creative, academic and professional communities.

However, as generative AI has evolved, the limitations of prompt engineering have become increasingly visible. It remains a valuable technique, especially for specialised tasks, but it no longer represents the dominant or even the most effective mode of human–AI interaction. Three developments are key to this shift.

© The Author(s), under exclusive license to Springer Nature Switzerland AG 2026
V. Geroimenko, *Communication Skills for Generative AI*, Human–Computer Interaction Series, https://doi.org/10.1007/978-3-032-21689-2_1

First, modern models have become far more conversational, contextual and adaptive. They no longer require rigid instruction patterns to operate effectively. Instead, they respond best to input that resembles natural communication: explanations of goals, descriptions of context, iterative clarification and collaborative refinement.

Second, AI interactions are moving well beyond text. Multimodal capabilities—speech, vision, audio, diagrams, tables, image editing, code execution and more—demand skills that encompass communication across multiple modes. The user is no longer merely 'engineering' a prompt but engaging in a rich, fluid exchange with an intelligent system capable of interpreting images, following complex workflows and integrating heterogeneous information sources.

Third, generative AI has entered the mainstream of daily life. Ordinary users—students, researchers, teachers, managers, administrators, clinicians and creative professionals—do not approach AI with a prompt engineer's mindset. They seek clarity, advice, explanation, ideas, solutions, analysis and collaboration. They naturally communicate using everyday language, narrative reasoning, analogies and forms of expression shaped by human-to-human conversation. This shift in expectations necessitates a corresponding shift in skills.

For these reasons, prompt engineering should now be understood as only one part of a far broader competence: *AI communication skills.* These skills involve understanding how the model perceives and interprets human input; how to provide context; how to shape the model's responses constructively; how to iterate productively; how to evaluate outputs critically; and how to collaborate with AI as an active cognitive partner rather than a passive machine.

This book argues that the future of human–AI interaction depends on expanding the conceptual framework beyond prompt engineering. Instead of focusing narrowly on instructions, users must learn to communicate with AI systems in a way that is natural, flexible, strategic and aligned with the cognitive and psychological principles of human communication. By treating AI as a partner in thinking, rather than a tool to be programmed, we open the door to more intuitive, efficient and meaningful forms of collaboration.

Thus, the shift from prompt engineering to comprehensive AI communication is not merely a refinement in technique—it is a transformation in how humans understand and work with intelligent systems. In the chapters that follow, we will explore why this transformation is necessary, how it is unfolding across domains of practice, and what new skills individuals and institutions must develop to thrive in an AI-enhanced world (Fig. 1.1).

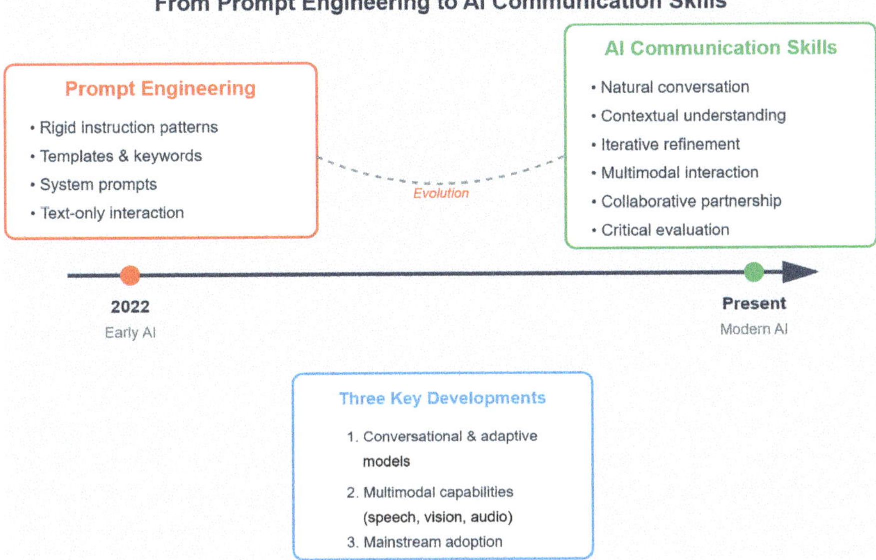

Fig. 1.1 The evolution from prompt engineering to AI communication skills. The transition from early prompt engineering (2022) to modern AI communication skills reflects three fundamental developments in human–AI interaction. Initial approaches relied on rigid templates and structured commands for text-based exchanges. Contemporary practice embraces natural conversation, iterative refinement, and multimodal capabilities. This evolution stems from: (1) increasingly conversational and adaptive AI models, (2) expanded multimodal interaction beyond text and (3) mainstream adoption requiring intuitive communication rather than technical engineering. The diagram illustrates how AI communication has transformed from a narrow technical skill into a broader, more naturalistic competence encompassing contextual understanding, collaborative partnership and critical evaluation

1.2 Why Generative AI Requires a New Human Competence

The rapid rise of generative AI represents a profound turning point in the history of human–computer interaction. For decades, people adapted to digital systems by learning fixed commands, rigid procedures and structured workflows. The burden was on the user to 'think like a computer' in order to operate software effectively. Generative AI reverses this relationship. For the first time, we are interacting with systems that can approximate elements of human reasoning, language use, creativity, and interpretive understanding. These systems do not simply execute instructions— they *participate* in meaning-making.

Because of this shift, generative AI requires a fundamentally new human competence, one that goes far beyond traditional digital literacy. The conventional skills of using a keyboard, navigating a graphical interface or operating standard software are no longer sufficient. What is now required is the ability to communicate with an intelligent system: to articulate intentions, provide context, frame problems, negotiate ambiguity and collaborate in the co-production of knowledge, ideas and solutions. This emerging competence is best understood as *AI communication literacy*.

Three developments explain why this new competence is indispensable.

First, generative AI operates through probabilistic interpretation rather than deterministic execution. Models do not follow precise commands in the way classical software does. Instead, they infer meaning, fill in gaps and generate responses shaped by context, prior turns, and the implicit cues within the user's language. Effective interaction, therefore, depends on the user's ability to express goals clearly, structure information intelligibly and manage ambiguity in a way that aligns with how the model interprets inputs.

Second, generative AI is increasingly embedded in high-stakes environments. AI is no longer confined to speculative or experimental settings; it now supports research, education, healthcare, governance, management, engineering and business operations. In these contexts, errors are not merely inconvenient—they can have real consequences. Users must therefore understand the limits of the systems they rely on and develop the communicative competence necessary to minimise misinterpretations, detect inconsistencies and guide AI output toward higher reliability and relevance.

Third, generative AI extends human cognitive capabilities in unprecedented ways. These systems provide analytical insight, creative support, summarisation, problem-solving, memory aids, multimodal reasoning and domain-specific expertise. To harness this potential, users must learn to articulate partial knowledge, describe intermediate steps and construct iterative dialogues that allow the AI to build upon—and improve—their own reasoning processes. In this respect, AI communication skills are not only technical but cognitive: they involve new habits of thinking and new strategies for co-creating meaning with a non-human partner.

This situation is historically unique. Previous technological revolutions required humans to adapt to new tools. The generative AI revolution requires humans to adapt to a new kind of *partner*—one that is capable of interpreting, shaping and generating information. Developing AI communication competence is therefore not optional but essential, both for individuals and for institutions aiming to thrive in a rapidly evolving technological landscape.

Later chapters of this book will explore the components of this competence in detail: context-setting, iterative refinement, multimodal communication, emotional and cognitive alignment, error detection and the cultivation of trust and transparency. But the foundation is clear: to work effectively with generative AI, humans must learn to communicate in ways that fully leverage the system's strengths while respecting its limitations. This new competence will define the next stage of human participation in an AI-rich world (Fig. 1.2).

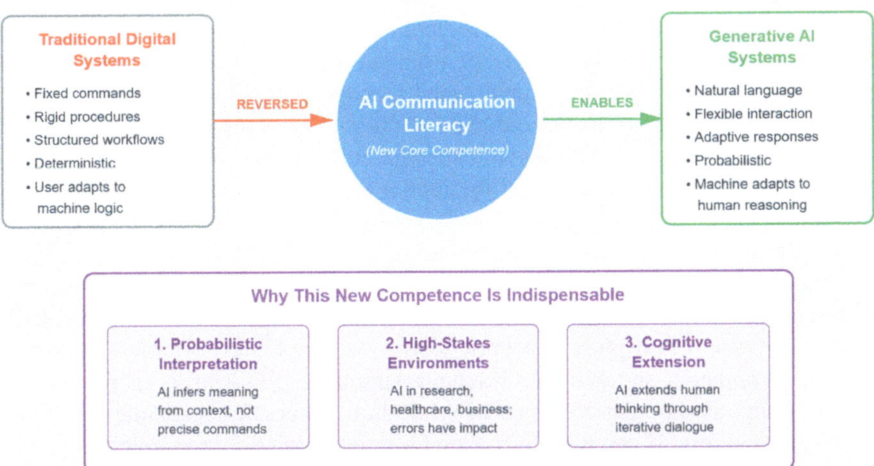

Fig. 1.2 The emergence of AI communication literacy as a core human competence. This diagram illustrates the fundamental shift in human–computer interaction brought about by generative AI. Traditional digital systems required users to adapt to machine logic through fixed commands and deterministic procedures. Generative AI reverses this relationship: machines now adapt to human reasoning through natural language and probabilistic interpretation. This reversal necessitates a new core competence—AI communication literacy—enabling effective interaction with intelligent systems. Three factors make this competence indispensable: (1) AI's probabilistic interpretation requiring contextual communication rather than precise commands, (2) deployment in high-stakes environments where errors have real consequences and (3) AI's role as a cognitive extension demanding iterative dialogue and collaborative reasoning

1.3 Everyday, Professional and Academic Use Cases

The growing presence of generative AI across all spheres of modern life illustrates how deeply these systems are becoming embedded in human activity. Their versatility enables them to support a remarkable range of tasks, from simple everyday queries to sophisticated professional and academic work. This breadth of application reveals not only the power of generative models but also the increasing importance of communicating with them effectively.

In daily life, people rely on AI for assistance with practical and routine matters: drafting messages, clarifying instructions, translating text, explaining unfamiliar concepts, organising schedules, generating ideas and offering guidance in uncertain situations. These interactions are conversational and informal, often resembling exchanges with a knowledgeable assistant. However, even seemingly simple interactions require clarity and context if the user expects helpful, accurate or personalised results. Ambiguous or incomplete requests frequently produce generic answers, showing that communication competence is essential even for everyday use.

In professional environments, generative AI now acts as a cognitive partner capable of supporting complex workflows. It assists in drafting reports, preparing analyses, evaluating data, reviewing documents, analysing risks, producing technical descriptions and generating creative or strategic ideas. In specialised fields—such as medicine, engineering, law, finance and management—it can synthesise information, propose interpretations and explore alternative scenarios. Yet professional settings often involve nuance, domain-specific constraints and high stakes. Misunderstandings between the user and the model can lead to errors with meaningful consequences. Communicating effectively, providing precise context and guiding the system towards reliable reasoning are therefore essential professional competencies.

Academic use cases are equally significant. Students employ AI to deepen understanding, clarify complex theories, analyse texts and develop academic writing skills. Researchers use it to explore concepts, design methodologies, examine arguments, propose hypotheses and generate literature summaries. Educators incorporate AI into teaching, assessment and curriculum design. Successful academic interaction requires the ability to ask well-formulated questions, set appropriate expectations, maintain intellectual standards and distinguish between well-supported information and model-generated speculation. Communicating effectively with AI, therefore, becomes part of academic literacy, supporting but not replacing critical thinking and scholarly judgement.

Across these varied domains, a common pattern emerges: generative AI becomes a meaningful collaborator only when the human user provides clear intentions, contextual information and constructive guidance. The diversity of use cases demonstrates that AI communication skills are no longer optional or confined to technical specialists. They have become essential for navigating everyday life, performing professional duties and participating in academic inquiry (Fig. 1.3).

1.4 Limits of Current Interaction Models

Although generative AI systems have advanced dramatically in their linguistic fluency, reasoning capabilities, and multimodal integration, the dominant models of human–AI interaction remain rooted in earlier paradigms that are increasingly inadequate for today's complex communication needs. For decades, human–computer interaction was designed around deterministic systems governed by precise commands, menu selections, templates and fixed workflows. Generative AI, by contrast, is probabilistic, adaptive and context-sensitive. Yet much of the world still approaches it using habits and expectations developed for traditional software. This mismatch between technical capability and human practice reveals several limitations that constrain the effectiveness, reliability and safety of AI-assisted work.

A fundamental limitation lies in the assumption that AI will simply 'understand' or 'figure out' what the user wants. Generative models are remarkably capable, but they do not possess true comprehension, shared experience, or a stable internal representation of the user's intent. Their interpretations depend on how information

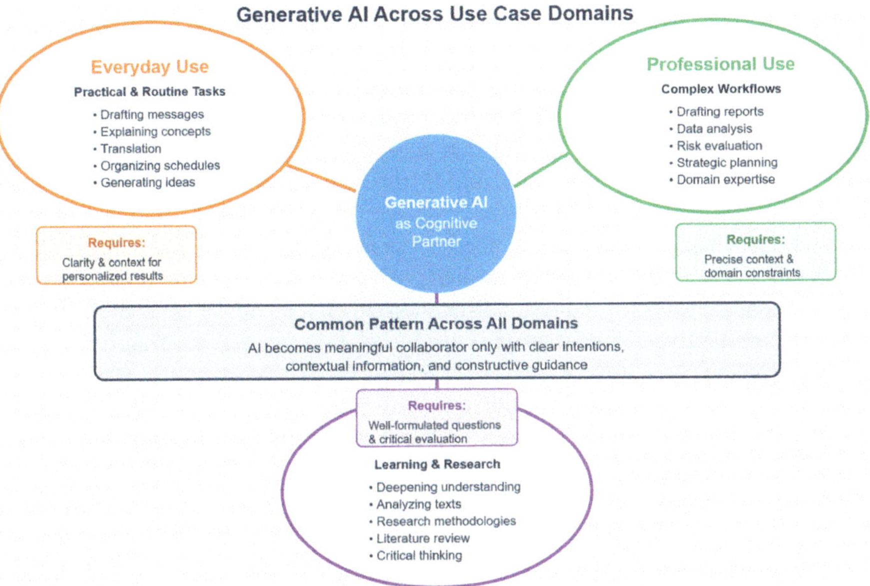

Fig. 1.3 Generative AI use cases: everyday, professional and academic domains. Generative AI functions as a cognitive partner across three primary domains of human activity. Everyday use encompasses practical tasks like drafting messages, explaining concepts and organising schedules, requiring clarity and context for personalised results. Professional use involves complex workflows, including report drafting, data analysis and strategic planning, that demand precise context and domain-specific constraints to manage high-stakes outcomes. Academic use supports learning and research through text analysis, methodology development and literature review, necessitating well-formulated questions and critical evaluation. Despite their diversity, all domains share a familiar pattern: AI becomes a meaningful collaborator only when users provide clear intentions, contextual information and constructive guidance throughout the interaction

is presented, how much context is provided, and how ambiguity is managed. When users rely on minimal instructions or assume that the system will infer their goals automatically, the model often fills gaps in unintended ways. This leads to generic answers, hallucinated details or responses that appear confident yet miss the core of the task. Many misunderstandings arise not from technical limitations but from an imprecise or unstructured communicative approach.

Another limitation is the persistence of transactional interaction patterns. Many users still treat generative AI as a tool that delivers a single answer in response to a single question, rather than as a conversation partner capable of iterative refinement. This mindset limits the potential for deeper reasoning, collaborative problem-solving and the gradual improvement of output quality through structured dialogue. When interaction remains transactional, users rarely correct assumptions, provide additional context or guide the system through logical steps. As a result, the AI generates outputs that may be superficially plausible but insufficiently aligned with the user's needs. Effective interaction requires a shift from one-shot commands to ongoing, constructive engagement.

A further limitation concerns the handling of uncertainty and error. Traditional software offers predictable behaviour: the same input always yields the same output. Generative AI does not operate in this manner. Its responses vary by phrasing, sequence of instructions and contextual history within the conversation. This variability can confuse users who expect deterministic reliability or who interpret stylistic confidence as evidence of factual accuracy. Moreover, many users do not yet possess the skills needed to evaluate AI-generated content critically, detect subtle inconsistencies, or request clarification when a response appears incomplete or overly speculative. Without these skills, interaction can become fragile and prone to misalignment.

There is also the challenge of cognitive mismatch. Humans communicate using rich background knowledge, implicit cultural cues, emotional nuance and shared assumptions that are not automatically accessible to an AI system. Meanwhile, AI models represent information statistically rather than conceptually, drawing on patterns across vast datasets rather than grounded understanding. When humans rely on implicit meaning or expect AI to recognise subtleties that are obvious to people, misinterpretation becomes likely. Successful communication requires the deliberate articulation of context, constraints and intentions—tasks that many users are not yet accustomed to performing explicitly.

Finally, existing interaction models often fail to account for the psychological dimensions of working with AI. Users may overtrust the system, assuming that its fluent language implies accuracy. Others may undertrust it, limiting their questions to trivial tasks and failing to explore its potential as a cognitive partner. Biases, expectations, anxieties and misunderstandings all influence how humans communicate with AI and how they interpret its output. Without awareness of these psychological factors, communication becomes inefficient and sometimes counterproductive.

These limitations reveal a clear gap between the behaviour of generative AI and the communicative habits of its users. As long as people rely on outdated interaction models, they will underutilise AI's capabilities and remain vulnerable to avoidable errors. The development of AI communication skills is therefore essential—not only for improving performance but also for reducing risks, enhancing clarity and fostering a more balanced, informed and effective partnership between humans and intelligent systems (Fig. 1.4).

1.5 Natural Communication as the New Paradigm

As generative AI becomes increasingly capable, accessible and integrated into daily life, a new paradigm of interaction is emerging—one grounded not in commands, templates or engineered phrasing but in natural, intuitive, conversational communication. The shift towards natural communication reflects a profound transformation in how humans approach intelligent systems, and it is reshaping expectations about what

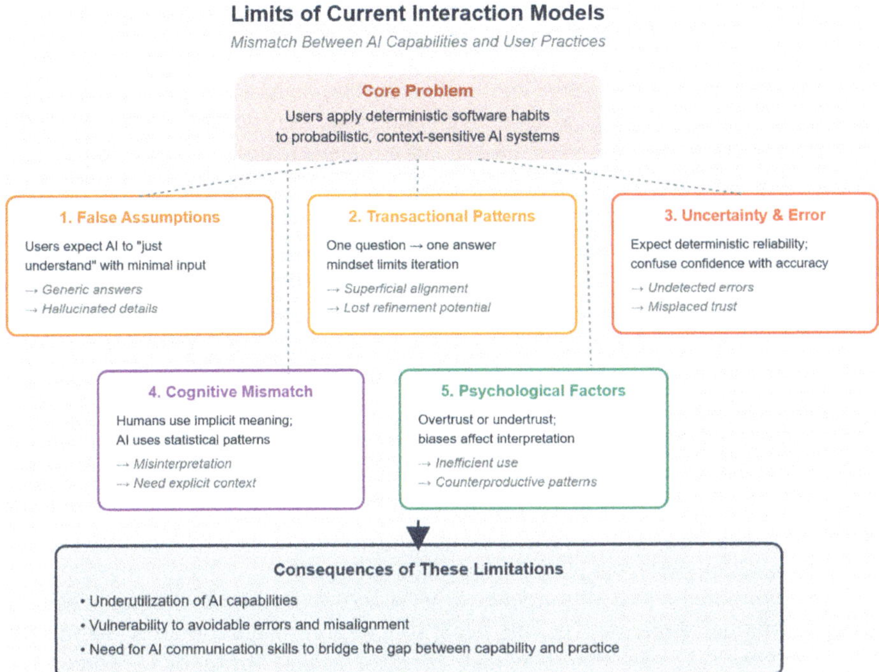

Fig. 1.4 Five critical limitations of current human–AI interaction models. Current interaction models suffer from a fundamental mismatch: users apply deterministic software habits to probabilistic, context-sensitive AI systems. Five key limitations emerge: (1) false assumptions that AI will automatically understand minimal input, leading to generic or hallucinated outputs; (2) transactional patterns treating AI as a one-shot answer provider rather than an iterative partner; (3) poor uncertainty handling, with users expecting deterministic reliability and confusing confident phrasing with accuracy; (4) cognitive mismatch between human implicit communication and AI's statistical pattern recognition; and (5) psychological factors including overtrust, undertrust, and interpretation biases. These limitations result in systematic underutilization of AI capabilities and vulnerability to avoidable errors, demonstrating the urgent need for comprehensive AI communication skills

effective interaction looks like. Rather than forcing users to adapt to the constraints of technology, modern AI invites technology to adapt to the fluidity and richness of human expression.

This paradigm shift is driven by the expanding linguistic and cognitive sophistication of generative models. Contemporary AI systems are increasingly able to interpret extended instructions, follow multi-step reasoning processes, incorporate contextual cues from earlier dialogue, and adapt to the user's style, preferences and goals. They can participate in iterative conversations, ask clarifying questions, summarise prior exchanges and maintain coherence over long interactions. These capabilities mean that AI responds most effectively not to rigid formulas but to communication that resembles real dialogue: explanations, examples, narratives, analogies and reflective thinking.

Natural communication with AI is not merely a matter of convenience. It is becoming essential for handling the complexity of modern tasks. Many activities that users rely on AI for—analysing problems, composing texts, planning projects, interpreting data, generating ideas or evaluating alternatives—are inherently multi-dimensional. They depend on nuance, context, interpretation and reasoning. Such tasks cannot be reduced to a simple command or a set of keywords. They require the expression of intention in a way that captures the user's perspective, priorities and background knowledge. Natural communication, with its flexibility and openness, provides the necessary structure for this kind of cognitive partnership.

One of the key features of this new paradigm is the growing expectation of recip-rocal collaboration. Natural communication assumes that the AI is not a passive executor but an active participant capable of contributing insight. Users increas-ingly approach AI as they would a colleague or assistant: providing background information, outlining constraints, asking for advice, exploring alternatives and refining ideas through dialogue. The interaction becomes a shared cognitive process in which both partners contribute to understanding and problem-solving. This collab-orative dynamic depends on communication practices that go beyond instruction and encompass explanation, negotiation and reflection.

The multimodal evolution of generative AI further reinforces the move towards natural communication. As systems begin to interpret images, analyse documents, recognise speech, create diagrams and integrate diverse forms of input, commu-nication expands beyond written text. Users can show rather than tell—providing photographs, sketches, screenshots, tables, recordings or spatial descriptions. They can combine these inputs with narrative explanations or questions. This blending of modalities mirrors how humans naturally communicate complex information and allows AI to engage with problems in a more holistic and intuitive way.

However, natural communication does not mean unstructured communication. Effective dialogue still requires clarity, intent, and thoughtful articulation. The capacity of AI to interpret human language does not absolve users of the responsi-bility to express their objectives or to manage ambiguity. Instead, the new paradigm shifts the focus from "engineering prompts" to cultivating communicative habits that align with how both humans and AI process information. This includes the ability to contextualise tasks, articulate constraints, provide examples, specify quality criteria, and revise expectations as the interaction unfolds.

The movement toward natural communication also has broader implications for education, professional practice and public life. It suggests that AI literacy is not primarily a technical skill but a communicative one. It highlights the importance of teaching people how to express ideas clearly, structure dialogue logically, eval-uate responses critically and engage constructively with an intelligent system. These skills are extensions of human-to-human communication but also adaptations to the distinctive characteristics of human–AI collaboration.

In this emerging paradigm, the most effective users are not those who memorise prompt templates but those who communicate with clarity, context and purpose. Natural communication becomes the bridge that enables generative AI to function as a genuine partner in thinking. As AI systems continue to evolve toward greater

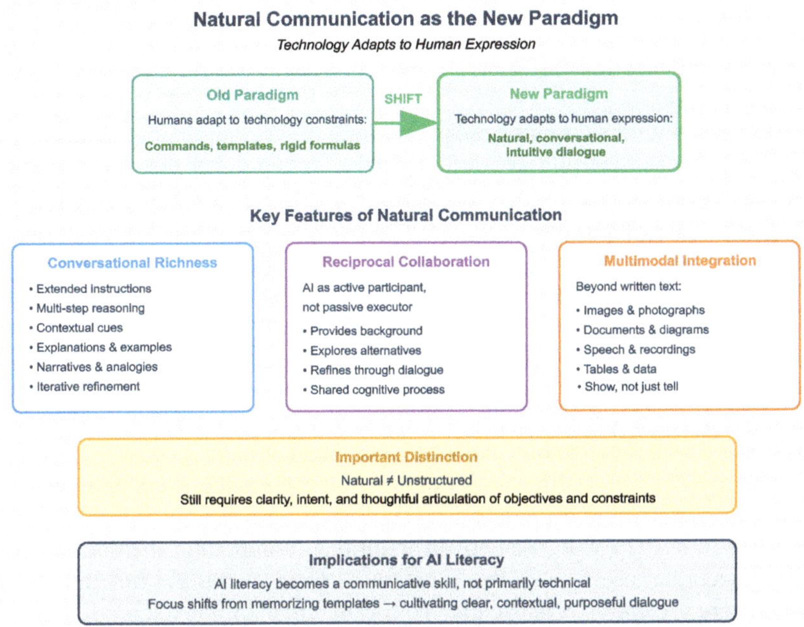

Fig. 1.5 The paradigm shift to natural communication in human–AI interaction. The emerging paradigm represents a fundamental reversal: rather than humans adapting to technology through rigid commands and templates, technology now adapts to human expression through natural, conversational dialogue. This shift is characterized by three key features: (1) conversational richness enabling extended instructions, multi-step reasoning, narratives, and iterative refinement; (2) reciprocal collaboration treating AI as an active cognitive partner in shared problem-solving rather than a passive executor; and (3) multimodal integration allowing users to communicate through images, documents, speech, and data—showing rather than just telling. Critically, natural communication does not mean unstructured communication; it still requires clarity, intent and thoughtful articulation. This paradigm redefines AI literacy as fundamentally a communicative skill, shifting focus from memorising prompt templates to cultivating clear, contextual and purposeful dialogue

contextual awareness, emotional intelligence and multimodal fluency, this paradigm will only gain in importance, shaping the next generation of tools and the next generation of human communicators (Fig. 1.5).

1.6 Towards the Psychology of Communicating with AI

Understanding how humans communicate with generative AI requires more than technical insight into how the models operate. It also demands an exploration of the psychological processes that shape interaction: the expectations users bring, the cognitive strategies they employ, the emotions they experience, and the mental models they construct to make sense of an intelligent but non-human partner. As generative AI continues to evolve, these psychological factors become central to effective communication, influencing both the quality of the interaction and the outcomes it produces.

A starting point for examining the psychology of AI communication is the recognition that humans naturally anthropomorphise systems that display competence, fluency or responsiveness. When an AI responds with coherent language, follows instructions or appears to reason, users often interpret these behaviours through the lens of human cognition. They may attribute understanding, intention or awareness to the system even when none is present. This tendency can lead to overtrust—accepting AI outputs uncritically—or misplaced expectations about what the system can and cannot do. At the same time, anthropomorphism can also facilitate smoother interaction, as users find it easier to communicate with systems that behave in familiar, conversational ways. Understanding and managing these psychological dynamics is essential for developing healthy, balanced communication practices.

Another psychological dimension lies in the mental models users develop to interpret AI behaviour. Mental models are simplified representations that help people predict how a system will respond. In traditional computing, mental models are relatively accurate: users know that a button performs a specific function or that a software feature behaves consistently. With generative AI, mental models are more complex and often less accurate. Because AI behaviour is probabilistic and context-dependent, users may struggle to understand why the system responded in a particular way or how to influence its behaviour consistently. This uncertainty can create confusion or frustration, especially when the AI produces answers that are superficially plausible but incorrect. Developing effective mental models—grounded in an understanding of how generative systems interpret inputs—becomes a key component of AI communication literacy.

Emotional factors also play a significant role. Users may feel excitement, curiosity or empowerment when interacting with AI, especially when the system helps them achieve tasks more efficiently or creatively. At the same time, they may feel anxiety, vulnerability, or intimidation when confronting a system that appears more knowledgeable than they are. These emotional states influence how people ask questions, how openly they explore ideas, and how they interpret feedback. For some, AI becomes a supportive partner that enhances confidence; for others, it becomes a source of pressure or dependence. Successful communication requires an emotional balance in which users feel empowered to engage with the system critically, without excessive reliance or undue scepticism.

The psychology of AI communication is also shaped by expectations of transparency and trust. Users want to understand the basis of the AI's responses, especially in professional or academic contexts where accuracy and accountability matter. When the system does not explain its reasoning or cannot provide clear evidence for its claims, users may lose confidence in the interaction. Trust, therefore, becomes contingent on the AI's ability to communicate transparently—and on the human's ability to question, verify, and assess the credibility of the output. Trust is not static;

it must be negotiated continuously through clear dialogue, critical reflection, and mutual alignment of goals.

Cognitive load presents another important consideration. Generative AI can simplify complex tasks, but it can also complicate them when users must repeatedly clarify instructions, correct errors, or evaluate long outputs. Poorly structured interaction increases cognitive effort, making communication inefficient or fatiguing. Effective communication strategies—such as breaking tasks into steps, establishing context early, and iteratively refining goals—help reduce cognitive load by making the dialogue more coherent and predictable. Teaching users these strategies is essential for enabling sustained, productive engagement with AI systems.

Finally, effective AI communication involves metacognition: the ability to reflect on one's own thinking and to monitor the quality of the interaction. Users must assess whether their request is clear, whether the AI's response meets the intended purpose, and whether additional context or constraints are needed. This form of self-awareness is crucial for steering the dialogue toward more precise and useful outcomes. It transforms interaction from a passive consumption of AI output into an active, reflective process of co-creation.

Taken together, these psychological factors reveal that communicating with AI is not merely a technical skill but a cognitive and emotional practice. It requires awareness of the limitations of AI, realistic expectations, well-calibrated trust and the ability to manage one's own communicative strategies. As generative AI becomes more deeply embedded in society, these psychological competencies will become increasingly important. They form the foundation for responsible, effective and meaningful collaboration in an era where humans and intelligent systems work together through language, ideas and shared reasoning (Fig. 1.6).

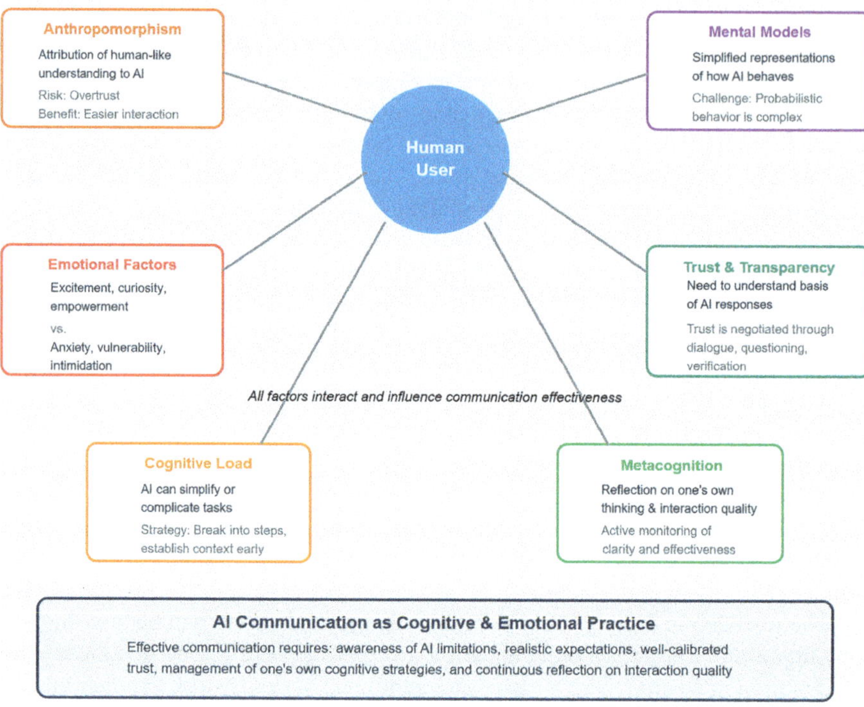

Fig. 1.6 Six psychological dimensions of human–AI communication. Effective AI communication transcends technical competence and requires sophisticated cognitive and emotional capabilities. Six interrelated psychological factors shape interaction quality: (1) anthropomorphism—the natural tendency to attribute human-like understanding to AI, risking overtrust while facilitating intuitive engagement; (2) mental models—simplified representations of probabilistic AI behaviour that users develop to predict system responses; (3) emotional factors—ranging from empowerment and curiosity to anxiety and intimidation, influencing how openly users engage; (4) trust and transparency—the need to understand response foundations, with trust negotiated through continuous dialogue and verification; (5) cognitive load—the mental effort required for interaction, managed through strategic structuring and context-setting; and (6) metacognition—reflective awareness of one's own thinking and interaction quality. Together, these dimensions reveal AI communication as fundamentally a cognitive and emotional practice demanding awareness of limitations, realistic expectations, calibrated trust, and active self-monitoring

Bibliography

1. Amershi, S., Weld, D., Vorvoreanu, M., et al.: Guidelines for Human–AI Interaction. In: Proceedings of CHI Conference on Human Factors in Computing Systems. ACM, New York, NY (2019)
2. Bahree, A.: Generative AI in Action. Manning Publications, New York, NY (2024)

3. Bender, E.M., Koller, A.: Climbing Towards NLU: On Meaning, Form, and Understanding in the Age of Data. In: Proceedings of the 58th Annual Meeting of the Association for Computational Linguistics, pp. 5185–5198. ACL, Stroudsburg, PA (2020)

4. Brown, T.B., et al.: Language Models are Few-Shot Learners. arXiv preprint arXiv:2005.14165 (2020)

5. Brynjolfsson, E., McAfee, A.: The Second Machine Age: Work, Progress, and Prosperity in a Time of Brilliant Technologies. W.W. Norton, New York, NY (2014)

6. Carrigan, M.: Generative AI for Academics. SAGE Publications, London (2024)

7. Clark, H.H.: Using Language. Cambridge University Press, Cambridge (1996)

8. Dhamani, N., Engler, M.: Introduction to Generative AI: An Ethical, Societal, and Legal Overview. Manning Publications, New York, NY (2024)

9. Eliot, L.: Essentials of Prompt Engineering for Generative AI: Practical Advances in Artificial Intelligence and Machine Learning. LBE Press Publishing, New York, NY (2024)

10. Floridi, L., Chiriatti, M.: GPT-3: Its Nature, Scope, Limits, and Consequences. Minds Mach. 30, 681–694 (2020)

11. Geroimenko, V.: The Essential Guide to Prompt Engineering: Key Principles, Techniques, Challenges, and Security Risks, Springer, Cham (2025)

12. Geroimenko, V.: Beyond and After Prompt Engineering: The Future of AI Communication, Springer, Cham (2026)

13. Geroimenko, V. (ed.): Human-Computer Creativity: Generative AI in Education, Art, and Healthcare, Springer, Cham (2025)

14. Grudin, J.: From Tool to Partner: The Evolution of Human–Computer Interaction. Synthesis Lectures on Human-Centered Informatics, vol. 10(1). Morgan & Claypool, San Rafael, CA (2017)

15. Halevy, A., Norvig, P., Pereira, F.: The Unreasonable Effectiveness of Data. IEEE Intell. Syst. 24(2), 8–12 (2009)

16. Kahneman, D.: Thinking, Fast and Slow. Farrar, Straus and Giroux, New York, NY (2011)

17. Kaptelinin, V., Bannon, L.: Interaction Design Beyond the Product: Creating Technology-Enhanced Activity Spaces. In: Human–Computer Interaction, 30(2–3), 267–275 (2015)

18. Lee, M.K.: Understanding Perception of Algorithmic Decisions: Fairness, Trust, and Emotion in Response to Algorithmic Management. Comput. Support. Coop. Work 27, 157–190 (2018)

19. Marcus, G., Davis, E.: Rebooting AI: Building Artificial Intelligence We Can Trust. Pantheon Books, New York, NY (2019)

20. Norman, D.A.: The Design of Everyday Things, Revised edn. MIT Press, Cambridge, MA (2013)

21. OpenAI: GPT-4 Technical Report. arXiv preprint arXiv:2303.08774 (2023)

22. Reeves, B., Nass, C.: The Media Equation: How People Treat Computers, Television, and New Media Like Real People and Places. Cambridge University Press, Cambridge (1996)

23. Russell, S., Norvig, P.: Artificial Intelligence: A Modern Approach, 4th edn. Pearson, New York, NY (2021)

24. Schneider, J., Handali, S.: Trust in Automated Systems. In: Springer Handbook of Automation, pp. 1881–1897. Springer, Berlin (2023)

25. Shneiderman, B.: Human-Centered AI. Oxford University Press, Oxford (2022)

26. Sparks, R., Khosravi, H.: Explainable Generative AI in Education: Opportunities and Challenges. Comput. Educ. 195, 104743 (2024)

27. Suchman, L.A.: Plans and Situated Actions: The Problem of Human–Machine Communication. Cambridge University Press, Cambridge (1987)

28. Turing, A.M.: Computing Machinery and Intelligence. Mind 59(236), 433–460 (1950)

29. Waytz, A., Cacioppo, J.T., Epley, N.: Who Sees Human? The Stability and Importance of Individual Differences in Anthropomorphism. Perspect. Psychol. Sci. 5(3), 219–232 (2010)

30. Weizenbaum, J.: Computer Power and Human Reason: From Judgment to Calculation. W.H. Freeman, San Francisco, CA (1976)cx

Chapter 2
Foundations of Human–AI Communication

To develop effective communication skills for generative AI, it is first necessary to understand what communication with AI actually entails. Unlike earlier forms of human–computer interaction, generative AI does not merely execute predefined instructions but interprets human input, infers intent and generates responses shaped by context, prior dialogue and probabilistic reasoning. This chapter provides the conceptual groundwork for human–AI communication by distinguishing it from traditional interaction paradigms and by examining how generative systems process and respond to human language and multimodal input. Establishing clear mental models of AI behaviour, context handling and communicative limitations is essential for building productive, reliable and responsible human–AI collaboration. This chapter, therefore, lays the theoretical foundation for the practical principles and techniques of AI communication in the chapters that follow.

2.1 What Is Communication with AI?

Communication with generative AI refers to a fundamentally new form of human–machine engagement in which meaning is not merely transmitted through commands but emerges through interpretive exchange. Unlike traditional computing systems, which respond to predefined inputs with deterministic outputs, generative AI systems operate by interpreting human language probabilistically and generating responses that are shaped by context, prior interaction and inferred intent. As a result, interaction with such systems is better understood as communication rather than operation.

It is essential to clarify what is meant by 'communication' in this context. Communication with AI does not imply shared understanding, consciousness or intentionality. Generative AI systems do not comprehend meaning in a human sense, nor do they possess beliefs, goals or awareness. However, they are capable of producing language that is semantically coherent, contextually appropriate and responsive to conversational cues. From a functional perspective, this is sufficient to constitute communication: meaning is constructed and negotiated through the exchange, even though it is not experienced symmetrically by both participants.

This functional asymmetry distinguishes human–AI communication from human–human communication while still preserving key communicative features. The human participant brings intentions, evaluative judgment and responsibility for outcomes. The AI contributes generative capacity, linguistic fluency, pattern recognition and inferential breadth derived from its training. Communication unfolds through dialogue, clarification and refinement, rather than through the execution of isolated commands. The interaction is therefore collaborative in form, even if agency remains unevenly distributed.

A defining characteristic of communication with AI is its interpretive nature. Generative models do not follow instructions literally; they infer meaning from linguistic patterns, contextual signals and conversational history. Slight variations in phrasing, order or emphasis can significantly influence outcomes. This sensitivity makes communication with AI both powerful and fragile. When intentions are articulated clearly and context is provided effectively, the system can produce highly relevant and sophisticated responses. When input is vague, incomplete or ambiguous, the system may generate outputs that are plausible but misaligned with the user's goals.

Another distinguishing feature is the dialogical structure of AI communication. Unlike traditional software interaction, which is typically transactional and one-directional, communication with generative AI unfolds over multiple turns. Users can elaborate on their goals, respond to AI output, correct misunderstandings and guide the system toward improved results. Meaning is not fixed at the outset but evolves through interaction. This iterative process aligns more closely with human communicative practices than with classical models of computation.

At the same time, communication with AI requires a reconceptualisation of responsibility and control. Because generative AI produces language that appears confident and coherent, users may be tempted to attribute authority or understanding to the system. Effective communication, therefore, depends on maintaining an accurate mental model of the AI's capabilities and limitations. The human communicator must remain actively engaged, evaluating output critically and steering the dialogue as needed. Communication with AI is thus not a passive exchange but an active cognitive practice.

Understanding what communication with AI is—and what it is not—is foundational for developing effective AI communication skills. It establishes the shift from treating AI as a programmable tool to engaging with it as a communicative system that responds to meaning rather than commands. This conceptual shift underpins the principles, techniques and practices explored in the subsequent sections of this chapter and throughout the book (Fig. 2.1).

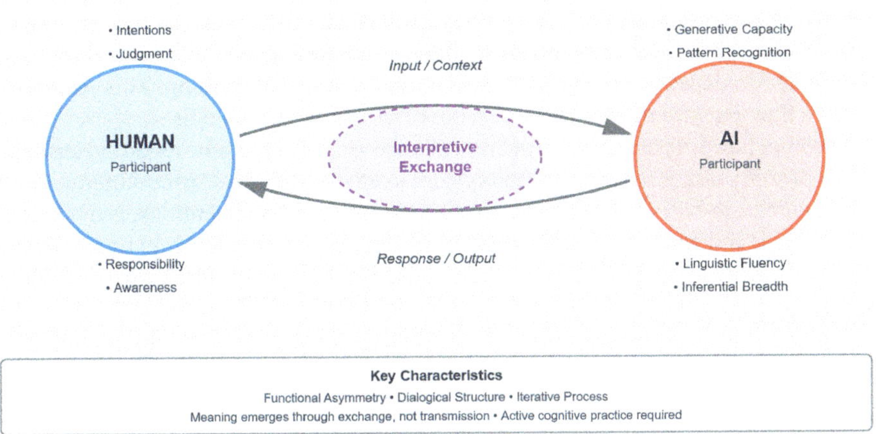

Fig. 2.1 Communication with AI: an interpretive exchange. This diagram illustrates the fundamental nature of human–AI communication as an asymmetric yet collaborative interpretive exchange. The human participant brings intentions, judgment, responsibility and awareness, while the AI contributes generative capacity, pattern recognition, linguistic fluency and inferential breadth. Communication unfolds through a bidirectional flow of input and response within an interpretive zone, characterised by functional asymmetry, dialogical structure and iterative processes. Meaning emerges through the exchange itself rather than through simple transmission, requiring active cognitive engagement on the part of the human communicator

2.2 Human–AI Interaction Versus Human–AI Communication

For much of the history of computing, the dominant paradigm governing human engagement with machines has been interaction rather than communication. Human–computer interaction (HCI) evolved around deterministic systems that required users to issue precise commands, select predefined options or follow structured workflows. In this paradigm, the computer is treated as a tool whose behaviour is predictable and whose responses are governed by explicit rules. Success depends on the user's ability to adapt to the system's logic and constraints.

Generative AI disrupts this paradigm fundamentally. Unlike traditional software, generative systems do not simply execute instructions. They interpret human input, probabilistically infer meaning and generate responses that are sensitive to context, phrasing and conversational history. This shift transforms engagement from interaction into communication. Instead of controlling a system through commands, users engage in an exchange of meaning in which outcomes emerge through dialogue.

The distinction between interaction and communication is not merely semantic; it reflects a bigger change in cognitive and operational dynamics. Human–AI interaction assumes stability and reproducibility: the same input yields the same output. Human–AI communication, by contrast, assumes variability and adaptation. Generative AI systems may respond differently to functionally similar inputs because interpretation depends on linguistic nuance and contextual framing. This variability is not a flaw but an inherent characteristic of probabilistic systems.

Another key difference lies in the role of the user. In interaction-based systems, the user's primary task is to learn how the system works and to issue correct commands. In communication-based systems, the user's task is to express intentions, provide relevant context and guide the system's interpretive process. Communicative competence replaces technical command knowledge as the central human skill. Clarity, structure and contextualisation become more important than syntactic precision.

This shift also alters how errors and misunderstandings arise. In traditional interaction, errors typically result from incorrect input or system malfunction. In human–AI communication, misalignment often stems from interpretive gaps: the AI infers a meaning different from the user's intent. Such misalignment is not always obvious, as generative systems can produce fluent and confident responses that appear plausible even when they diverge from the intended task. Detecting and correcting these misinterpretations requires ongoing communicative engagement rather than simple error correction.

Furthermore, interaction models emphasise interface design—buttons, menus and workflows—while communication models emphasise dialogue design. The quality of interaction depends less on the visual or procedural interface and more on the structure of the conversation itself. Effective communication involves establishing goals, negotiating assumptions, refining requests and iteratively improving outcomes. This places new demands on users, who must become active participants in shaping the dialogue rather than passive recipients of output.

The communicative paradigm also reshapes expectations of agency and collaboration. In interaction-based systems, agency resides almost entirely with the human user. In communication-based systems, agency is distributed asymmetrically. The human defines objectives and evaluates results, while the AI contributes generative exploration and linguistic realisation. This asymmetry requires careful calibration. Overestimating AI agency leads to overtrust, while underestimating it results in underutilisation of its capabilities.

Recognising the distinction between human–AI interaction and human–AI communication is therefore essential for effective and responsible use of generative AI. It explains why traditional HCI assumptions no longer suffice and why new communicative competencies are required. This shift provides the conceptual foundation for understanding how humans can engage productively with AI systems that are no longer merely tools but participants in meaning-oriented exchange (Fig. 2.2).

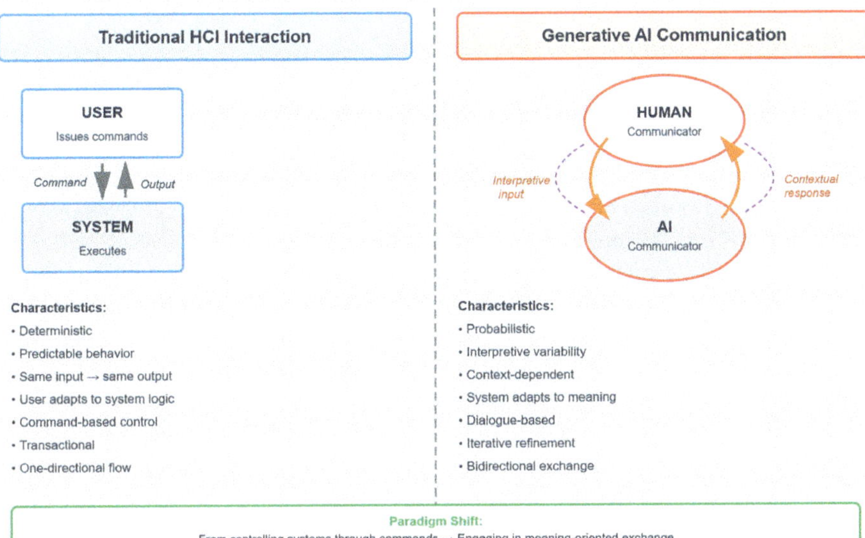

Fig. 2.2 From interaction to communication: a paradigm shift. This diagram demonstrates the fundamental shift from traditional human–computer interaction to human–AI communication. On the left, traditional HCI is characterised by deterministic, command-based exchanges where users issue instructions and systems execute predefined responses in a transactional, one-directional flow. On the right, generative AI communication is characterised by probabilistic, interpretive exchanges in which human and AI participants engage in bidirectional, context-dependent, iterative dialogue. The paradigm shift represents a move from controlling systems through commands to engaging in meaning-oriented exchange, where communication competence replaces technical command knowledge

2.3 How Generative Models Interpret Human Input

Effective communication with generative AI depends critically on understanding how these systems interpret human input. Unlike humans, generative models do not process language through conceptual understanding, lived experience or intentional reasoning. Instead, they rely on probabilistic inference, generating responses by estimating the most likely continuation of a given input based on patterns learned during training. This distinction has profound implications for how communication unfolds and why specific communicative strategies succeed or fail.

At a fundamental level, generative models treat human input as a sequence of tokens embedded in a contextual space. Interpretation emerges not from semantic comprehension but from statistical associations between linguistic forms and usage patterns observed across vast datasets. As a result, meaning is approximated rather than understood. The model does not 'know' what a request means; it infers the most appropriate response based on the structure, phrasing and contextual cues in the input. Communication is therefore shaped as much by how something is said as by what is said.

Context plays a decisive role in this interpretive process. Generative models rely heavily on surrounding information—previous dialogue turns, implicit assumptions and framing cues—to determine their responses. Input is never interpreted in isolation; it is always evaluated relative to an evolving conversational state. This explains why the same question can yield different answers depending on when it is asked, how it is phrased or what information preceded it. From a communicative perspective, interaction with AI is cumulative rather than episodic.

The probabilistic nature of interpretation also accounts for variability in output. Unlike deterministic systems, generative models do not guarantee identical responses to identical inputs. Minor linguistic changes—such as word choice, sentence structure or emphasis—can alter how the model infers intent and, consequently, how it responds. This variability is often surprising to users accustomed to traditional software behaviour, but it is a defining feature of generative systems. Communication with AI, therefore, requires tolerance for variation and strategies for guiding inference rather than enforcing control.

Another essential characteristic of generative interpretation is the absence of intrinsic truth evaluation. Models are optimised to produce plausible and coherent responses, not to verify factual accuracy or logical soundness. When input is underspecified, contradictory or ambiguous, the model may confidently generate content that appears authoritative but is poorly aligned with reality or the user's intent. Such responses are not errors in execution but predictable outcomes of probabilistic inference operating under uncertainty. Recognising this limitation is essential for responsible communication.

Generative models also lack stable internal representations of goals or commitments across interactions unless explicitly reinforced. They do not retain intentions in the way humans do, nor do they monitor consistency over time unless prompted to do so. As a result, users must take an active role in maintaining coherence by restating objectives, clarifying constraints and correcting misinterpretations as they arise. Communication becomes an ongoing process of alignment rather than a single act of instruction.

Understanding how generative models interpret input enables users to communicate more effectively and critically. It shifts expectations away from literal obedience and toward interpretive collaboration. Users who recognise that AI output reflects inferred meaning rather than understanding are better equipped to structure requests, manage ambiguity and evaluate responses appropriately. This awareness forms a key component of AI communication literacy and prepares the ground for developing productive mental models of AI behaviour, which is the focus of the next section (Fig. 2.3).

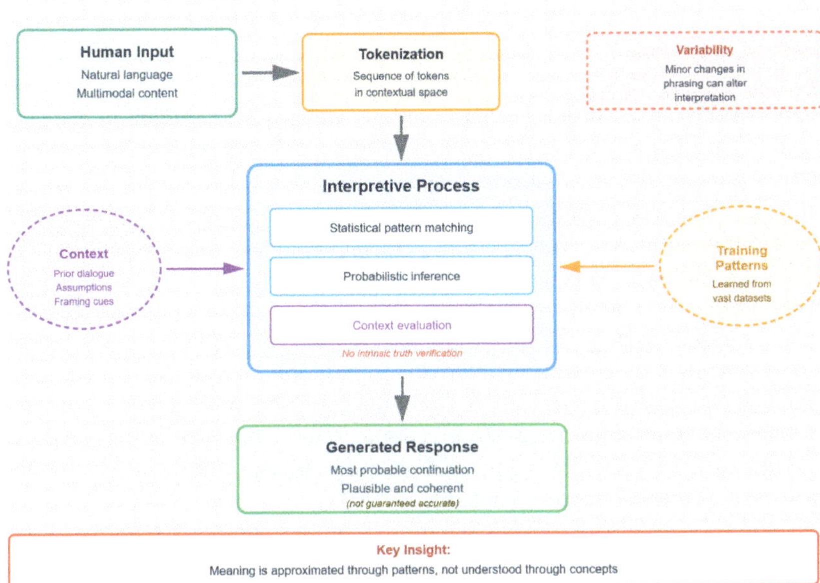

Fig. 2.3 Generative AI: probabilistic interpretation process. This diagram shows how generative AI systems interpret human input through a probabilistic process rather than conceptual understanding. Human input undergoes tokenisation into sequences embedded in contextual space, which then enters an interpretive process involving statistical pattern matching, probabilistic inference and context evaluation. Two key influences shape this process: contextual information (prior dialogue, assumptions and framing cues) and patterns learned from vast training datasets. The system lacks intrinsic mechanisms for verifying truth, producing responses that represent the most probable continuation—plausible and coherent, but not guaranteed to be accurate. Minor variations in phrasing can significantly alter interpretation outcomes

2.4 Mental Models for Communicating with AI

Mental models play a decisive role in how humans communicate with generative AI systems. A cognitive model is an internal representation that people use to understand how a system works, anticipate its behaviour and guide their interactions with it. When mental models are accurate, communication becomes efficient and purposeful. When they are flawed or incomplete, interaction often leads to confusion, misplaced trust or underutilisation of the system's capabilities.

Many difficulties in human–AI communication stem not from technical limitations of generative models but from inappropriate mental models held by users. A common misconception is to treat generative AI as a search engine that retrieves information from a fixed database. This model encourages short, keyword-based queries and leads to frustration when the system produces interpretive or synthetic responses rather than definitive facts. Another widespread mental model frames AI as a human expert or authority figure, leading users to accept fluent responses uncritically and to attribute understanding, intention or accountability to the system. Such assumptions can lead to overtrust and the unexamined adoption of incorrect or biased outputs.

Equally problematic is the opposite extreme: viewing AI as an unreliable novelty or a purely mechanical tool with limited relevance. Users who adopt this mental model tend to restrict interaction to trivial tasks and fail to engage in the iterative dialogue required to unlock the system's generative and analytical potential. In both cases, communication is shaped—and constrained—by expectations that do not reflect how generative AI actually operates.

More productive mental models conceptualise AI as a cognitive partner or reasoning support system. In this view, the AI does not replace human judgment but complements it by generating alternatives, exploring possibilities, summarising information and supporting reflection. Communication becomes a process of steering and refinement rather than command execution. The human user defines goals, evaluates outcomes and remains responsible for decisions, while the AI contributes linguistic fluency and inferential breadth.

Developing such mental models requires an understanding of both the strengths and limitations of generative AI. These systems excel at pattern recognition, synthesis and variation across domains, but they lack grounded understanding, intentional reasoning and intrinsic verification mechanisms. Recognising these characteristics helps users calibrate trust appropriately. Rather than asking whether an AI response is 'right' or 'wrong' in absolute terms, effective communicators ask whether it is plausible, relevant and aligned with the intended purpose—and then verify as needed.

Mental models also influence how users manage ambiguity and error. Users who expect deterministic behaviour may interpret variability as failure, while those who understand probabilistic inference recognise it as an opportunity for exploration and refinement. By adjusting their mental models, users can shift from frustration to collaboration, treating unexpected responses as signals that additional clarification or context is required.

Importantly, mental models are not static. They evolve through experience, reflection and education. Explicit instruction in how generative AI systems function can accelerate this process, enabling users to form more accurate expectations and to communicate more strategically. This is why mental model formation is a central component of AI communication literacy and should be addressed explicitly in educational and professional contexts.

Ultimately, effective communication with AI depends as much on how users think about the system as on what they say to it. Mental models shape communicative behaviour, influence trust and responsibility, and determine whether AI is approached as a tool, an authority, or a collaborative partner. Cultivating appropriate mental models is therefore essential for enabling productive, ethical and effective human–AI communication (Fig. 2.4).

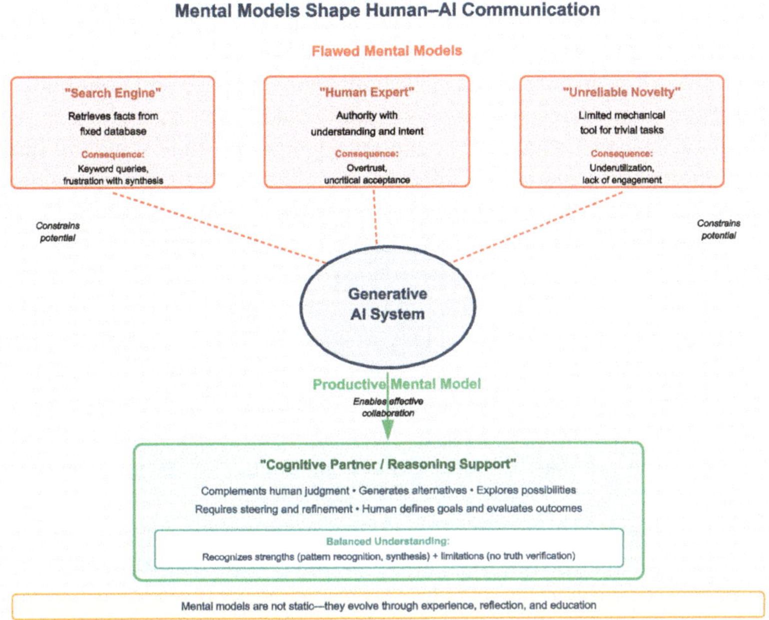

Fig. 2.4 Mental models shape human–AI communication. This diagram depicts how different mental models fundamentally shape the quality of human–AI communication. Three flawed mental models are shown: treating AI as a 'search engine' leads to keyword queries and frustration with synthesis; viewing it as a 'human expert' results in overtrust and uncritical acceptance; and perceiving it as an 'unreliable novelty' leads to underutilization and disengagement. In contrast, the productive mental model conceptualises AI as a 'cognitive partner' or reasoning support system that complements human judgment, requires steering and refinement, and balances recognition of both strengths (pattern recognition, synthesis) and limitations (no truth verification). Mental models are not static but evolve through experience, reflection and education

2.5 The Role of Context, Memory and Multimodality

Context is the central mechanism through which meaning is constructed in human–AI communication. Generative AI systems do not interpret input in isolation; they rely on contextual information to infer intent, relevance and scope. Context includes explicit instructions, background information, constraints, examples and the dialogue's accumulated history. The quality of AI output is therefore strongly dependent on how effectively this contextual frame is established and maintained throughout the interaction.

Unlike humans, generative AI systems do not possess long-term memory or shared experiential knowledge unless explicitly designed to retain information across sessions. In most cases, their operational 'memory' is limited to the current interaction window. This constraint has significant communicative implications. Users cannot assume that the system will remember earlier goals, preferences or decisions unless these are reintroduced or reinforced. Effective communication thus requires deliberate context management, including summarising objectives, restating constraints and re-establishing priorities as conversations evolve.

The absence of persistent memory also affects coherence and continuity. When context is lost or diluted, the system may produce responses that are locally plausible but globally inconsistent with earlier intentions. Users who understand this limitation are better equipped to maintain alignment by carefully structuring dialogue and recognising when contextual reinforcement is needed. Context management becomes a core communicative skill rather than a background assumption.

Multimodality further expands the role of context in human–AI communication. Contemporary generative AI systems increasingly support input and output across multiple modalities, including text, images, documents, tables, diagrams and audio. This capability allows users to communicate complex information in ways that more closely resemble human communicative practices. Visual material can convey spatial relationships, patterns or design intent more efficiently than text alone, while textual explanation can clarify purpose and constraints that images cannot express independently.

However, multimodal communication also introduces new challenges. Generative AI does not automatically infer how different inputs relate to one another or which aspects are most relevant to the task. Users must therefore provide explicit guidance on how to interpret multimodal inputs and how to integrate them into the response. Without such guidance, the system may focus on irrelevant features or misinterpret the intended relationship between modalities.

The interplay between context, memory and multimodality highlights the shift from issuing isolated requests to orchestrating coherent exchanges. Communication becomes an active process of alignment in which users continuously shape the interpretive environment within which the AI operates. This process requires planning, reflection and adaptability—skills that go beyond traditional notions of digital literacy.

Contextual awareness also has implications for responsibility and evaluation. Because generative AI responds to the context it is given, users share responsibility for the output's relevance and quality. Poorly framed context can lead to misleading or inappropriate responses, while well-constructed context enables more accurate and valuable outcomes. Recognising this shared responsibility encourages a more reflective and ethical approach to AI communication.

As generative AI systems continue to evolve toward richer contextual awareness and more seamless multimodal integration, the importance of these communicative skills will only increase. The ability to manage context deliberately, compensate for limited memory and integrate multiple forms of input effectively will define successful human–AI collaboration. These competencies form a bridge between foundational understanding and the practical principles of AI communication explored in the next chapter (Fig. 2.5).

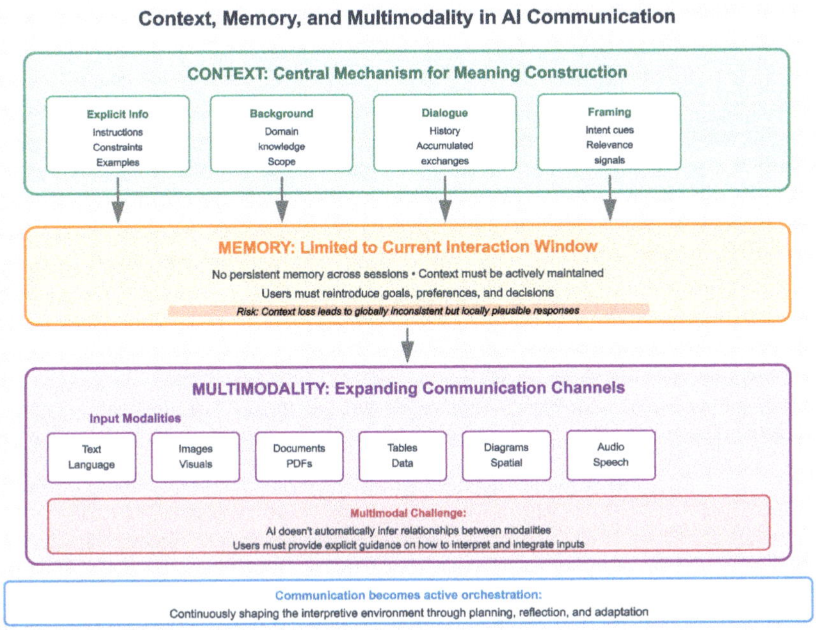

Fig. 2.5 Context, memory and multimodality in AI communication. This diagram explains the three critical dimensions that shape effective human–AI communication. At the top, context serves as the central mechanism for meaning construction, encompassing explicit information, background knowledge, dialogue history and framing cues. The middle layer highlights a critical constraint: AI memory is limited to the current interaction window, requiring users to actively maintain context by reintroducing goals and preferences, with the risk that context loss leads to locally plausible but globally inconsistent responses. The bottom layer shows multimodality's expansion of communication channels through text, images, documents, tables, diagrams and audio, while noting the challenge that AI does not automatically infer relationships between modalities. Effective communication requires users to continuously orchestrate these elements through planning, reflection and adaptation

Bibliography

1. Bahree, A.: Generative AI in Action. Manning Publications (2024)
2. Brown, T.B., et al.: Language Models are Few-Shot Learners. arXiv preprint arXiv:2005.14165 (2020).
3. Carrigan, M: Generative AI for Academics. SAGE Publications Ltd (2024).
4. Dhamani, N., Engler, M.: Introduction to Generative AI: An Ethical, Societal, and Legal Overview. Manning Publications (2024)
5. Eliot, L.: Essentials of Prompt Engineering for Generative AI: Practical Advances in Artificial Intelligence and Machine Learning. LBE Press Publishing (2024).
6. Feuerriegel, S., Hartmann, J., Janiesch, C., et al.: Generative AI. Bus Inf Syst Eng 66, 111–126 (2024). https://doi.org/10.1007/s12599-023-00834-7
7. Gao, T., et al.: Making Pre-trained Language Models Better Few-shot Learners. arXiv preprint arXiv:2012.15723 (2020).

8. Geroimenko, V.: The Essential Guide to Prompt Engineering: Key Principles, Techniques, Challenges, and Security Risks, Springer, Cham (2025)
9. Geroimenko, V.: Beyond and After Prompt Engineering: The Future of AI Communication, Springer, Cham (2026)
10. Geroimenko, V. (ed.): Human-Computer Creativity: Generative AI in Education, Art, and Healthcare, Springer, Cham (2025)
11. GitHub: Prompt Engineering Guide. https://github.com/dair-ai/Prompt-Engineering-Guide. Accessed 20 Oct 2024.
12. Greenwood, M.: Artificial Intelligence: A Practical Guide to Using AI in Everyday Life. Ochreland Publishing (2024).
13. Hunter, N.: The Art of Prompt Engineering with ChatGPT: A Hands-on Guide. AI Press (2023).
14. Khan, I.: The Quick Guide to Prompt Engineering. Wiley (2024).
15. Learn Prompting. https://learnprompting.org. Accessed 15 Oct 2024.
16. Liu, P., et al.: Pre-train, Prompt, and Predict: A Systematic Survey of Prompting Methods in Natural Language Processing. arXiv preprint arXiv:2107.13586 (2021).
17. OpenAI: Best Practices for Prompt Engineering with the OpenAI API. https://help.openai.com/en/articles/6654000-best-practices-for-prompt-engineering-with-the-openai-api. Accessed 18 Oct 2024.
18. Phoenix, J., Taylor, M.: Prompt Engineering for Generative AI. O'Reilly Media (2024).
19. Prompt Engineering Guide. https://www.promptingguide.ai/. Accessed 7 Oct 2024.
20. Prompt Engineering Holy Grail. https://promptengineeringhub.dev/. Accessed 8 Oct 2024.
21. Radford, A., et al.: Learning Transferable Visual Models from Natural Language Supervision. arXiv preprint arXiv:2103.00020 (2021).
22. Rothman, D.: Transformers for Natural Language Processing and Computer Vision: Explore Generative AI and Large Language Models with Hugging Face, ChatGPT, GPT-4V, and DALL-E 3. Packt Publishing (2024).
23. Schick, T., Schütze, H.: Exploiting Cloze-Questions for Few-Shot Text Classification and Natural Language Inference. arXiv preprint arXiv:2001.07676 (2020).
24. Shin, J., Tang, C., Mohati, T., Nayebi, M., Wang, S., Hemmati, H.: Prompt Engineering or Fine Tuning: An Empirical Assessment of Large Language Models in Automated Software Engineering Tasks. arXiv preprint arXiv:2310.10508 (2023).
25. Sibal, A.: Hands-On Prompt Engineering: Learning to Program ChatGPT Using OpenAI APIs. Wiley (2025).
26. Vairamani, A.D., Nayyar, A.: Prompt Engineering: Empowering Communication. CRC Press (2024).
27. Zhou, D., et al.: Large Language Models are Human-Level Prompt Engineers. arXiv preprint arXiv:2211.01910 (2022)

Chapter 3
The Core Principles of Communicating with Generative AI

Having established the foundations of human–AI communication, this chapter turns to the principles that govern effective and responsible dialogue with generative AI systems. While generative models can produce fluent, contextually responsive output, the quality of the interaction depends critically on how humans communicate with them. The chapter articulates a set of core principles that guide users in expressing intent, structuring dialogue, managing uncertainty and maintaining cognitive and ethical oversight. These principles do not prescribe specific techniques or templates; rather, they define enduring communicative norms that support productive collaboration with AI across domains. By framing AI communication as a principled human skill rather than a technical procedure, the chapter prepares the reader for the practical strategies explored in the chapters that follow.

3.1 Clarity, Specificity and Structure

Clarity, specificity and structure form the foundational principles of effective communication with generative AI. While these qualities are central to human communication more broadly, they acquire heightened importance in human–AI dialogue due to the interpretive and probabilistic nature of generative models. Unlike human interlocutors, AI systems cannot rely on shared experience, implicit understanding, or contextual intuition beyond what is explicitly or cumulatively provided. As a result, the communicative burden shifts decisively towards the human user.

Clarity in AI communication refers to the explicit expression of intent. Generative models infer meaning from linguistic patterns rather than conceptual understanding, so vague or loosely formulated requests often yield generic, misaligned or overly broad outputs. Clear communication requires articulating what is being asked, why it is being asked and what kind of response is expected. This does not mean excessive detail, but rather intentional articulation. When users clarify objectives early, they reduce ambiguity and guide the model's inferential process towards more relevant outcomes.

Specificity complements clarity by narrowing the interpretive space in which the AI operates. Generative models are designed to explore possibilities; without constraints, they tend to default to generalised or conventional responses. Specificity provides boundaries that shape generation. These boundaries may involve scope, audience, format, level of depth, assumptions or constraints. Importantly, specificity is not about controlling every detail but about identifying what matters most. Well-chosen constraints increase relevance and reliability without undermining flexibility.

Structure plays a critical role in translating clarity and specificity into interpretable input. Generative AI systems are sensitive not only to content but also to organisation. Information presented in a logical sequence—goals first, followed by context, constraints and expectations—supports more accurate interpretation. Even when detailed, poorly structured input can overwhelm or mislead the model by obscuring priorities. Structured communication helps the AI distinguish between primary objectives and supporting information.

These three principles operate synergistically. Clarity defines purpose, specificity defines boundaries and structure defines relationships. When one is absent, the effectiveness of the others is diminished. An explicit but unstructured request may still produce scattered results. A specific but unclear request may constrain the model in unintended ways. A well-structured request without clarity of intent may be internally coherent but externally misaligned.

The importance of these principles becomes especially apparent in complex or multi-step tasks. When users ask AI to analyse, evaluate, compare or generate extended content, the system must infer not only the topic but also the intended cognitive operation. Explicitly stating whether the task involves explanation, critique, synthesis, or exploration significantly improves alignment. Similarly, indicating the desired level of detail or formality prevents mismatches between user expectations and AI output.

It is also essential to recognise that clarity, specificity and structure are not static qualities applied once at the beginning of an interaction. In communicative dialogue, they are refined iteratively. Users may begin with a broad request, assess the AI's response and then clarify or restructure subsequent input. This iterative sharpening reflects effective communication practice rather than initial failure. Skilled users treat early responses as probes that reveal how the model is interpreting their intent.

Finally, these principles underscore a central theme of this book: effective AI communication is not about learning special commands but about cultivating communicative discipline. The skills required—articulating intent, structuring information and defining constraints—are extensions of human communicative competence, adapted to a non-human interlocutor. Mastery of clarity, specificity and structure lays the foundation for all other AI communication principles and techniques (Fig. 3.1).

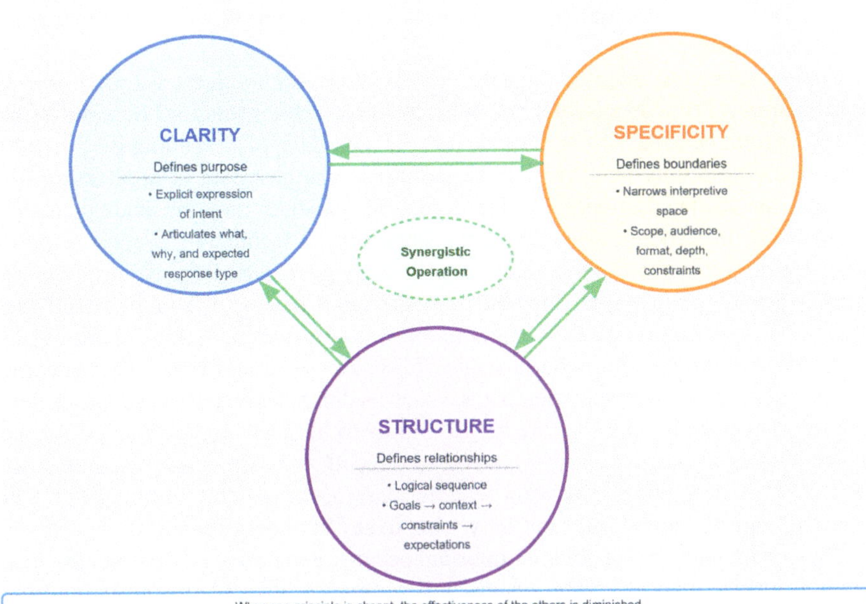

Fig. 3.1 Three foundational principles of AI communication. This diagram depicts the three synergistic principles that form the foundation of effective AI communication: clarity, specificity and structure. Clarity defines purpose by explicitly expressing intent and articulating what is being asked and why. Specificity defines boundaries by narrowing the interpretive space through constraints such as scope, audience, format and depth. Structure defines relationships by organising information in logical sequences that support accurate interpretation. The bidirectional arrows between all three principles demonstrate their synergistic operation, emphasising that when one principle is absent, the effectiveness of the others is diminished

3.2 Intent, Purpose and Outcome Orientation

Effective communication with generative AI requires more than clarity of expression; it requires intentionality. At the same time, clarity focuses on how a request is articulated, intent and purpose address why the interaction is taking place and what the user ultimately seeks to achieve. Generative AI systems are highly responsive to linguistic form, but they do not inherently distinguish between goals unless those goals are explicitly or implicitly communicated. As a result, users who fail to articulate intent often receive responses that are linguistically appropriate yet strategically misaligned.

Intent in human–AI communication refers to the underlying objective that motivates a request. This may include seeking an explanation, generating ideas, evaluating alternatives, exploring possibilities or producing a concrete artefact. Humans routinely infer intent in everyday conversation through shared context, social cues and prior knowledge. Generative AI lacks access to these inferential resources. It can only approximate intent based on patterns in the input. When intent is not made explicit, the model may default to a generic interpretation that does not match the user's actual goal.

Closely related to intent is purpose, which situates the request within a broader context of use. Purpose answers questions such as: Who is this for? In what setting will the output be used? What constraints or standards apply? Without purpose, AI-generated output may be correct in isolation but inappropriate in application. For example, an explanation suitable for a general audience may be inadequate in a professional or academic context. At the same time, a technically precise response may be unsuitable for communication with non-specialists. Purpose provides the situational grounding that enables the model to tailor its response more effectively.

Outcome orientation extends intent and purpose into expectations about results. It involves communicating what a successful response should look like. Outcome-oriented communication specifies criteria such as depth, format, tone, scope, or decision relevance. Rather than asking the AI simply to 'explain' or 'analyse', outcome-oriented users indicate what they intend to do with the response—whether it will inform a decision, support writing, enable learning or generate alternatives. This framing helps the model infer not only what to say but how to say it.

These principles are especially important because generative AI does not independently prioritise relevance. The system will generate a plausible response to almost any request, regardless of whether that response meaningfully advances the user's goals. When intent and purpose are underspecified, the AI may satisfy the surface requirements of the request while missing its functional objective. Communicating intent and expected outcomes reduces this risk by narrowing the space of plausible interpretations.

Intent, purpose and outcome orientation also play a critical role in iterative communication. As dialogue unfolds, users may refine or revise their goals in response to AI output. Making these shifts explicit—by restating intent or adjusting desired outcomes—helps maintain alignment across turns. Without such recalibration, conversations may drift, producing outputs that are coherent locally but disconnected from the user's evolving objectives.

Importantly, intent-oriented communication reinforces human agency and responsibility. By articulating goals and evaluating outcomes, users maintain control over the direction and use of AI-generated content. This guards against passive reliance on the system and supports reflective engagement. The AI contributes generative capability, but the human defines success.

In human–AI communication, then, effective dialogue is not driven solely by what is asked, but by why it is requested and what the user hopes to achieve. Making intent, purpose and desired outcomes explicit transforms AI interaction from a reactive exchange to a goal-directed collaboration. This principle forms a critical bridge between foundational understanding and the iterative communicative practices explored in the sections that follow (Fig. 3.2).

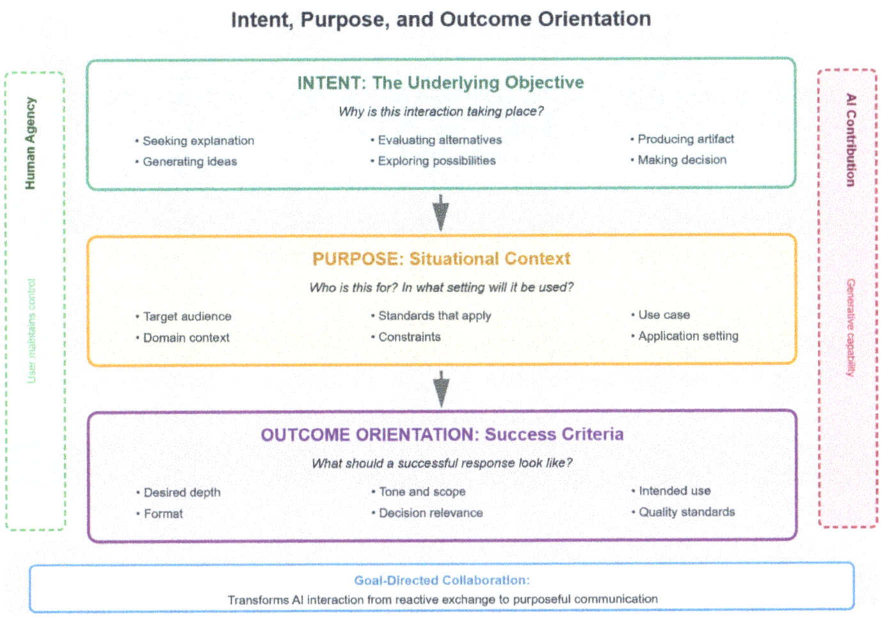

Intent, Purpose, and Outcome Orientation

Fig. 3.2 Intent, purpose and outcome orientation. This diagram shows the three-layered framework of intentional communication with generative AI. The top layer represents intent, addressing why the interaction is taking place and the underlying objective (seeking explanation, generating ideas, evaluating alternatives). The middle layer depicts purpose, which situates the request within a broader context by identifying the target audience, the domain context and applicable standards. The bottom layer presents an outcome-oriented approach, specifying success criteria, including desired depth, format, tone and intended use. Human agency is maintained throughout the process while AI contributes generative capability, transforming interaction from reactive exchange to goal-directed collaboration

3.3 Iteration and Refinement as Communication Norms

Iteration and refinement are not signs of failure in communication with generative AI; they are defining features of effective dialogue. Unlike traditional software systems, which are designed to produce a correct output from a single, well-formed input, generative AI systems operate through probabilistic interpretation and contextual inference. As a result, meaningful communication with AI is inherently iterative. Understanding this shift is essential for developing realistic expectations and productive communicative practices.

In human–human communication, meaning is often refined through conversation. Speakers clarify their intentions, address misunderstandings and adjust their language based on feedback. Human–AI communication follows a similar pattern, but with significant differences. Generative AI does not possess awareness of misunderstanding unless it is made explicit, nor does it independently seek clarification unless prompted. The responsibility for refinement, therefore, rests primarily with the human user. Iteration becomes the mechanism through which alignment is achieved.

Early exchanges in an AI dialogue often function as exploratory probes. A user may present a preliminary request to gauge how the system interprets the task. The AI's reponse reveals implicit assumptions, interpretive choices and areas of misalignment. Rather than accepting or rejecting this output outright, effective communicators treat it as feedback. They refine subsequent input by clarifying goals, narrowing scope, correcting assumptions or adjusting constraints. Through this process, communication evolves towards greater precision and relevance.

Refinement also supports cognitive offloading and shared reasoning. Users may begin with incomplete or loosely formed ideas and rely on the AI to help structure them. As the dialogue progresses, the user's understanding becomes clearer and the AI's output becomes more targeted. This reciprocal shaping of thought and response transforms interaction into a collaborative cognitive process. Iteration enables users to externalise thinking, test alternatives and progressively converge on a satisfactory outcome.

A critical aspect of iterative communication is the explicit acknowledgement of adjustment. Users who state how or why they are refining a request—by indicating what worked, what did not, or what needs to change—provide valuable context for the AI's interpretive process. Such metacommunicative signals help maintain coherence and reduce drift across turns. Without them, refinement may appear arbitrary to the system, weakening alignment.

Iteration also plays a key role in managing uncertainty and error. Because generative AI can produce confident but flawed responses, users must actively assess output quality and request correction or elaboration when needed. Iterative questioning, rephrasing and verification are essential safeguards against misinterpretation and hallucination. This process reinforces the human's role as evaluator and decision-maker, counterbalancing the AI's fluency with critical judgement.

Importantly, iteration should be understood as a norm rather than an exception. Users who expect immediate perfection from a single prompt often experience frustration or misalignment. By contrast, those who approach communication as a dynamic process are better able to adapt to the system's strengths and limitations. Iterative engagement reduces cognitive load by distributing problem-solving across multiple conversational turns rather than attempting to anticipate every requirement upfront.

Finally, recognising iteration as a communicative norm has educational and professional implications. It suggests that effective AI communication skills involve not only formulating reasonable initial requests but also developing the ability to listen, evaluate and respond strategically. These skills resemble those used in human–human dialogue and extend naturally to human–AI collaboration.

Iteration and refinement thus constitute a core principle of AI communication. They enable alignment, support reasoning and transform generative AI from a one-shot response generator into a partner in an evolving communicative process (Fig. 3.3).

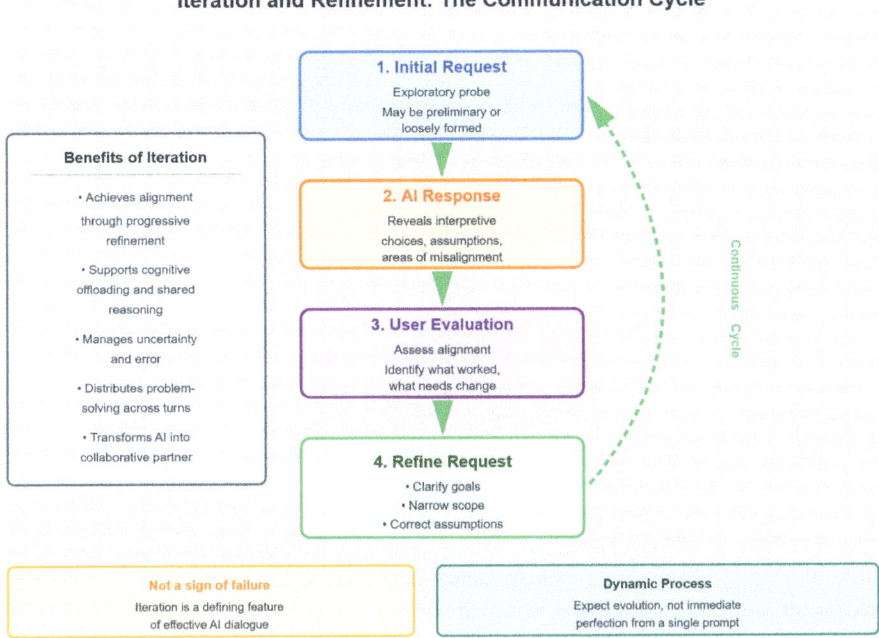

Fig. 3.3 Iteration and refinement: the communication cycle. This diagram explains iteration and refinement as the defining features of effective AI dialogue rather than signs of failure. The cyclical process begins with an initial request serving as an exploratory probe, followed by an AI response that reveals interpretive choices and assumptions. Users then evaluate the response to assess alignment and identify needed changes, leading to refined requests that clarify goals, narrow scope and correct assumptions. This continuous cycle enables progressive alignment, supports cognitive offloading and shared reasoning, manages uncertainty and error and transforms AI from a one-shot response generator into a collaborative partner in an evolving communicative process

3.4 Cognitive Alignment and Transparency

Cognitive alignment refers to the degree to which a generative AI system's responses correspond to the user's intentions, assumptions, reasoning processes and expectations. In human–AI communication, alignment is not automatic. It must be actively constructed and maintained through transparent communication practices that make goals, assumptions and reasoning explicit. Without such alignment, interaction may remain superficially fluent while failing to support the user's actual cognitive needs.

One of the central challenges in communicating with generative AI is the mismatch between human reasoning and AI inference. Humans reason conceptually, drawing on lived experience, causal understanding and shared cultural knowledge. Generative AI, by contrast, operates through statistical associations and pattern-based inference. While this enables impressive linguistic fluency, it also means the system may produce responses that appear logically coherent but are not grounded in the user's intended frame of reference. Cognitive alignment, therefore, requires users to externalise aspects of their thinking that would otherwise remain implicit in human-to-human communication.

Transparency is the primary mechanism for achieving alignment. Transparent communication involves articulating assumptions, intermediate steps, evaluation criteria and uncertainties. When users explain not only what they want but how they are thinking about the task, they provide the AI with a richer interpretive framework. This reduces the risk of misalignment by narrowing the gap between inferred intent and actual intent. Transparency does not require exhaustive detail, but it does require intentional disclosure of what matters cognitively.

Cognitive alignment is critical in analytical, evaluative, or creative tasks. When users ask AI to analyse an argument, compare alternatives, or generate ideas, the quality of the output depends heavily on the implicit standards being applied. Without transparency, the AI must guess which criteria are relevant—depth versus breadth, originality versus accuracy, exploration versus decision support. Explicitly stating these priorities allows the system to generate responses that are more closely aligned with the user's reasoning goals.

Transparency also plays a crucial role in managing trust. Generative AI systems often produce confident-sounding output, which can obscure uncertainty or speculation. Users who request transparency—such as asking the AI to explain its reasoning, outline assumptions or acknowledge limitations—gain greater visibility into how conclusions are constructed. This visibility supports critical evaluation and helps prevent overreliance on output that may be plausible but weakly supported. Transparency thus functions as both a communicative and an epistemic safeguard.

Cognitive alignment is not a one-time achievement but an ongoing process. As dialogue progresses, the user's goals may evolve, new constraints may emerge, or initial assumptions may be revised. Maintaining alignment requires continuous adjustment through clarification and feedback. When misalignment occurs, effective communicators address it explicitly by identifying where the AI's reasoning diverged from their intent and by restating priorities or constraints. This metacommunicative practice reinforces alignment and keeps the dialogue productive.

It is also essential to recognise that perfect alignment is neither realistic nor necessary. Generative AI is inherently limited by its lack of genuine understanding and by the probabilistic nature of its responses. The goal of cognitive alignment is not to eliminate all divergence but to manage it constructively. Small misalignments can stimulate reflection or reveal alternative perspectives, while larger misalignments signal the need for clarification or reframing.

Ultimately, cognitive alignment and transparency reinforce the human's active role in AI communication. They shift interaction away from passive consumption of output towards deliberate collaboration. By making reasoning explicit and by requesting clarity from the system, users engage AI as a cognitive partner rather than an authority. This principle strengthens both the effectiveness and the responsibility of human–AI communication, preparing the ground for the ethical considerations addressed in the next section (Fig. 3.4).

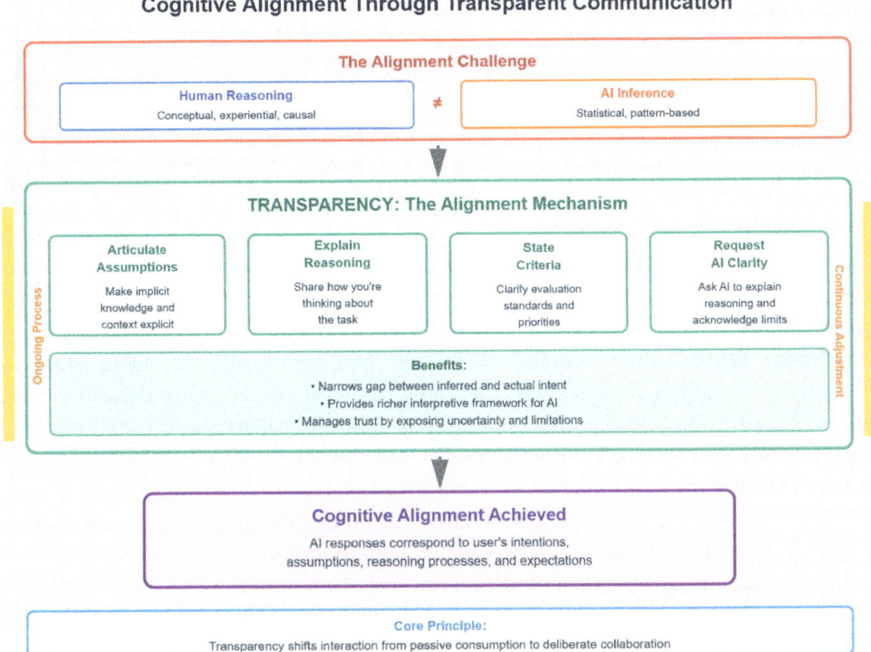

Fig. 3.4 Cognitive alignment through transparent communication. This diagram compares the fundamental mismatch between human reasoning (conceptual, experiential, causal) and AI inference (statistical, pattern-based), then presents transparency as the primary mechanism for achieving cognitive alignment. Four key transparency practices are shown: articulating assumptions to make implicit knowledge explicit, explaining reasoning processes, stating evaluation criteria and priorities and requesting clarity from AI about its reasoning and limitations. These practices narrow the gap between inferred and actual intent, provide richer interpretive frameworks and manage trust by exposing uncertainty. The diagram emphasises that alignment is an ongoing process requiring continuous adjustment rather than a one-time achievement

3.5 Ethical and Responsible AI Communication

Ethical and responsible communication with generative AI is not a separate or optional concern; it is an integral dimension of effective human–AI interaction. Because generative AI systems participate in meaning-making and influence human decisions, the way users communicate with them has ethical consequences. These consequences arise not only from what the AI produces but from how humans frame requests, interpret responses and integrate AI-generated content into real-world contexts.

A central ethical issue in AI communication is responsibility. Generative AI does not possess moral agency, intention, or accountability. Responsibility for the use, interpretation and consequences of AI-generated output remains with the human user. Ethical communication, therefore, begins with recognising this asymmetry. Users must resist the temptation to treat AI output as authoritative or to defer judgement to the system. Communicating responsibly means maintaining critical oversight, verifying claims where appropriate and taking ownership of decisions informed by AI assistance.

Transparency is closely linked to responsibility. Ethical AI communication requires openness about the role AI plays in a given task. In academic, professional and public contexts, users may have an obligation to disclose AI involvement, particularly when AI-generated content influences decisions, assessments, or published material. Transparent communication with AI—requesting explanations, acknowledging uncertainty and understanding limitations—supports transparent communication with others about how AI has been used.

Another ethical dimension concerns bias and representation. Generative AI systems are trained on large datasets that reflect existing social, cultural and historical biases. As a result, AI-generated content may reproduce stereotypes, omit perspectives, or privilege dominant viewpoints. Ethical communication involves awareness of these tendencies and the ability to challenge or correct them through deliberate framing and critical evaluation. Users who communicate responsibly do not treat AI output as neutral or objective but as situated and contingent.

Intentional misuse also raises ethical concerns. Generative AI can be prompted to produce misleading, manipulative, or harmful content if users frame requests accordingly. Ethical communication, therefore, includes a commitment to appropriate use. This does not require detailed technical knowledge of AI safeguards but does require reflective judgement about the purposes to which AI is applied. Communicating ethically with AI means aligning requests with broader human values such as fairness, accuracy, respect and social responsibility.

Ethical considerations also extend to dependency and autonomy. As generative AI becomes more capable, users may be tempted to offload judgement, creativity or decision-making excessively. Responsible communication maintains human agency by using AI as support rather than substitution. This involves asking questions that stimulate thinking rather than replace it and treating AI-generated suggestions as inputs to reflection rather than conclusions. Ethical communication preserves the human's role as thinker, author and decision-maker.

In professional and educational contexts, ethical AI communication intersects with standards of practice and integrity. Communicating responsibly with AI includes understanding what forms of AI assistance are appropriate in a given domain and how they align with institutional norms. It also involves teaching and modelling responsible communicative behaviour so that AI literacy includes ethical awareness alongside technical competence.

Finally, ethical AI communication is forward-looking. As generative AI systems continue to evolve, communicative practices established today will shape future norms of human–AI collaboration. By emphasising responsibility, transparency, critical engagement and respect for human values, users contribute to a culture of ethical AI use that extends beyond individual interactions.

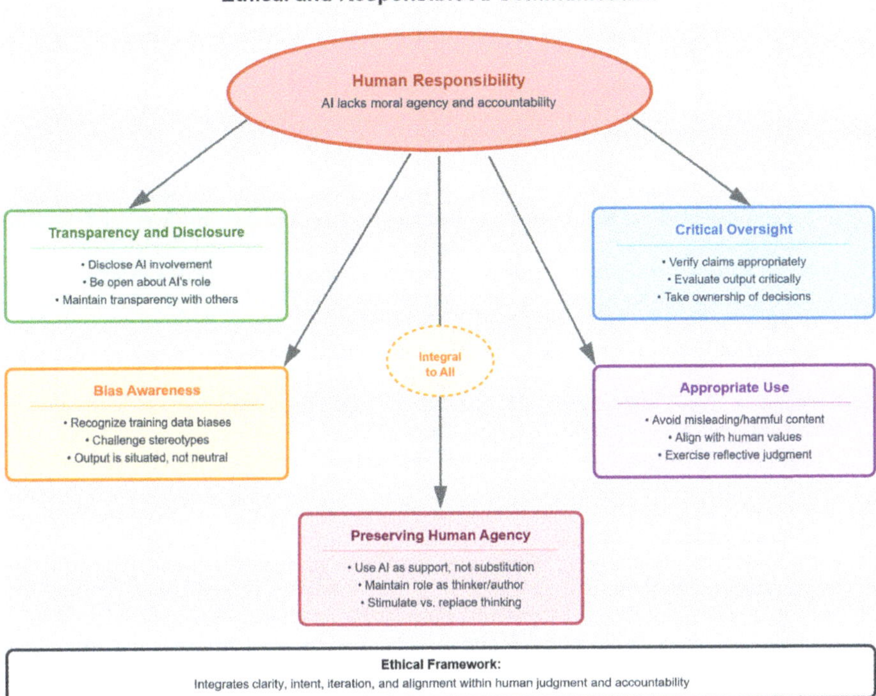

Fig. 3.5 Ethical and responsible AI communication. This diagram presents the five integral dimensions of ethical AI communication radiating from the central principle of human responsibility. Since AI lacks moral agency and accountability, humans must maintain: (1) transparency and disclosure about AI's role in decisions and outputs, (2) critical oversight through verification and evaluation, (3) bias awareness to recognise and challenge stereotypes reproduced from training data, (4) appropriate use aligned with human values and reflective judgement and (5) preservation of human agency by using AI as support rather than substitution. These dimensions integrate with the other core principles of clarity, intent, iteration and alignment to form a comprehensive ethical framework grounded in human judgement and accountability

Ethical and responsible communication thus completes the core principles of AI communication. It integrates clarity, intent, iteration and alignment within a framework of human judgement and accountability. Together, these principles define not only how to communicate effectively with generative AI but also how to do so in ways that support trust, integrity and meaningful human agency (Fig. 3.5).

Bibliography

1. Amatriain, X.: Prompt Design and Engineering: Introduction and Advanced Methods. arXiv preprint arXiv:2401.14423 (2024).

2. Anthropic's Documentation: Build with Claude - Prompt Engineering Overview. https://docs.anthropic.com/en/docs/build-with-claude/prompt-engineering/overview. Accessed 11 Oct 2024.

3. Chen, B., Zhang, Z., Langrené, N., Zhu, S.: Unleashing the Potential of Prompt Engineering in Large Language Models: A Comprehensive Review. arXiv preprint arXiv:2310.14735 (2023).

4. Codecademy: Learn Prompt Engineering Course. https://www.codecademy.com/learn/learn-prompt-engineering. Accessed 5 Nov 2024.

5. dair.ai: Prompt Engineering Guide. https://www.promptingguide.ai. Accessed 12 Nov 2024.

6. DeepLearning.AI: ChatGPT Prompt Engineering for Developers. https://www.deeplearning.ai/short-courses/chatgpt-prompt-engineering-for-developers/. Accessed 24 Oct 2024.

7. Eliot, L.: Essentials of Prompt Engineering for Generative AI: Practical Advances in Artificial Intelligence and Machine Learning. LBE Press Publishing (2024).

8. Fernando, C., Banarse, D.S., Michalewski, H., Osindero, S., Rocktäschel, T.: Promptbreeder: Self-Referential Self-Improvement via Prompt Evolution. arXiv preprint arXiv:2402.12345 (2024).

9. Geroimenko, V.: The Essential Guide to Prompt Engineering: Key Principles, Techniques, Challenges, and Security Risks, Springer, Cham (2025)

10. Geroimenko, V.: Beyond and After Prompt Engineering: The Future of AI Communication, Springer, Cham (2026)

11. Geroimenko, V. (ed.): Human-Computer Creativity: Generative AI in Education, Art, and Healthcare, Springer, Cham (2025)

12. GitHub: Prompt Engineering Repository. https://github.com/NirDiamant/Prompt_Engineering. Accessed 2 Oct 2024.

13. Hunter, N.: The Art of Prompt Engineering with ChatGPT: A Hands-on Guide. AI Press (2023).

14. Kansal, A.: Prompt Engineering Techniques. In: Building Generative AI-Powered Apps. Apress, Berkeley, CA (2024). https://doi.org/10.1007/979-8-8688-0205-8_8

15. Khan, I.: The Quick Guide to Prompt Engineering. Wiley (2024).

16. LambdaTest: Prompt Engineering Tutorial. https://www.lambdatest.com/learning-hub/prompt-engineering. Accessed 24 Nov 2024.

17. Learn Prompting: https://learnprompting.org. Accessed 13 Nov 2024.

18. Linzbach, S., Dimitrov, D., Kallmeyer, L., Evang, K., Jabeen, H.: Quantifying Language Models' Sensitivity to Spurious Features in Prompt Design. arXiv preprint arXiv:2407.00123 (2024).

19. Marvin, G., Hellen, N., Jjingo, D., Nakatumba-Nabende, J.: Prompt Engineering in Large Language Models. In: Jacob, I.J., Piramuthu, S., Falkowski-Gilski, P. (eds) Data Intelligence and Cognitive Informatics. ICDICI 2023. Algorithms for Intelligent Systems. Springer, Singapore (2024) https://doi.org/10.1007/978-981-99-7962-2_30

20. McTear, M., Ashurkina, M.: Advanced Prompt Engineering. In: Transforming Conversational AI. Apress, Berkeley, CA (2024). https://doi.org/10.1007/979-8-8688-0110-5_6

21. OpenAI Help Center: Best Practices for Prompt Engineering with the OpenAI API. https://help.openai.com/en/articles/6654000-best-practices-for-prompt-engineering-with-the-openai-api. Accessed 5 Oct 2024.

22. OpenAI: Prompt Engineering Documentation. https://platform.openai.com/docs/guides/prompt-engineering. Accessed 16 Oct 2024.

23. Phoenix, J., Taylor, M.: Prompt Engineering for Generative AI. O'Reilly Media (2024).

24. Polo, F.M., Xu, R., Weber, L., Silva, M., Bhardwaj, O.: Efficient Multi-Prompt Evaluation of LLMs. arXiv preprint arXiv:2410.12345 (2024).

25. Pryzant, R., Iter, D., Li, J., Lee, Y.T., Zhu, C.: Automatic Prompt Optimization with "Gradient Descent" and Beam Search. arXiv preprint arXiv:2302.12345 (2023).

26. Sahoo, P., Singh, A.K., Saha, S., Jain, V., Mondal, S., Chadha, A.: A Systematic Survey of Prompt Engineering in Large Language Models: Techniques and Applications. arXiv preprint arXiv:2402.07927 (2024).

27. Sclar, M., Choi, Y., Tsvetkov, Y., Suhr, A.: Quantifying Language Models' Sensitivity to Spurious Features in Prompt Design. arXiv preprint arXiv:2407.00123 (2024).

28. Sibal, A.: Hands-On Prompt Engineering: Learning to Program ChatGPT Using OpenAI APIs. Wiley (2025).
29. Singh, B.: Magic of Prompt Engineering. In: Building Applications with Large Language Models. Apress, Berkeley, CA (2024). https://doi.org/10.1007/979-8-8688-0569-1_4
30. Singh, C., Morris, J., Aneja, J., Rush, A., Gao, J.: Explaining Patterns in Data with Language Models via Interpretable Autoprompting. arXiv preprint arXiv:2210.03493 (2022).
31. Soh, J., Singh, P.: Prompt Engineering Techniques, Small Language Models, and Fine-Tuning. In: Data Science Solutions on Azure. Apress, Berkeley, CA (2024). https://doi.org/10.1007/979-8-8688-0914-9_6
32. Unite.AI: Prompt Engineering Courses. https://www.unite.ai/prompt-engineering-courses/. Accessed 18 Oct 2024.
33. Vairamani, A.D., Nayyar, A.: Prompt Engineering: Empowering Communication. CRC Press (2024).
34. Wahle, J.P., Ruas, T., Xu, Y., Gipp, B.: The Language of Prompting: What Linguistic Properties Make a Prompt Successful? In: Proceedings of the 2023 Conference on Empirical Methods in Natural Language Processing (EMNLP 2023), pp. 1234–1245. Association for Computational Linguistics, 2023.
35. Ye, Q., Axmed, M., Pryzant, R., Khani, F.: Prompt Engineering a Prompt Engineer. arXiv preprint arXiv:2311.05661 (2023).
36. Bozkurt, A.: Tell Me Your Prompts and I Will Make Them True: The Alchemy of Prompt Engineering and Generative AI. Open Praxis 15(1), 23-34 (2023).
37. Wahle, J.P., Ruas, T., Xu, Y., Gipp, B.: The Language of Prompting: What Linguistic Properties Make a Prompt Successful? In: Proceedings of the 2023 Conference on Empirical Methods in Natural Language Processing (EMNLP 2023), pp. 1234–1245. Association for Computational Linguistics, 2023.

Chapter 4
Essential Techniques for Effective AI Interaction

Having established the foundational concepts and core principles of human–AI communication, this chapter focuses on practical techniques for effective interaction with generative AI systems. These techniques operationalise communicative principles such as clarity, intent, iteration and alignment, transforming them into repeatable strategies for guiding AI behaviour. The chapter moves beyond prompt engineering by presenting communication techniques that are adaptable across tasks, domains and modalities. By learning how to frame tasks, explore ideas collaboratively, manage context and constraints, structure dialogue iteratively and communicate across multiple modes, readers develop practical skills for working with AI as a responsive and reflective partner. These techniques provide the groundwork for understanding common communication failures and misalignments, which are examined in the next chapter.

4.1 Instructional Communication: Giving Clear Tasks

Instructional communication represents the most direct and widely used mode of interaction with generative AI. In this mode, the human user asks the system to perform a defined task: to explain, summarise, analyse, generate, transform or evaluate content. Although this form of communication appears straightforward, its effectiveness depends on how well the task is articulated. Poorly framed instructions often produce output that is fluent but misaligned, incomplete or unusable. Effective instructional communication, therefore, requires more than issuing commands; it requires translating human intent into communicative form that the AI can interpret reliably.

A defining challenge of instructional communication with generative AI lies in the system's interpretive nature. Generative models do not execute tasks in a literal sense. Instead, they infer the type of task being requested based on linguistic cues,

© The Author(s), under exclusive license to Springer Nature Switzerland AG 2026

V. Geroimenko, *Communication Skills for Generative AI*, Human–Computer Interaction Series, https://doi.org/10.1007/978-3-032-21689-2_4

structure and context. When instructions are underspecified, the system must guess which interpretation is most appropriate. This frequently results in generic responses that satisfy the surface form of the request but do not address its underlying purpose. Instructional communication succeeds when the task is framed in a way that reduces interpretive ambiguity.

Effective task-giving begins with explicit task definition. Rather than assuming the AI will infer what action is required, users benefit from clearly stating the communicative operation they expect. Explaining, analysing, comparing, synthesising, critiquing and generating are cognitively distinct tasks, yet they are often conflated in everyday language. Explicitly identifying the intended operation helps the AI align its response with the user's cognitive goal. This practice reflects a broader shift from implicit expectation to explicit articulation in human–AI communication.

Scope control is another essential element of instructional communication. Generative AI systems can produce output at varying levels of detail, abstraction and breadth. Without guidance, they often default to moderate generality. Effective instructions specify scope by indicating boundaries such as length, depth, audience or focus. Importantly, scope control does not require micromanagement. It involves identifying what should be included or excluded so that the system's generative capacity is directed toward what matters most.

Instructional communication also benefits from contextual anchoring. Tasks rarely exist in isolation; they are embedded within broader goals or workflows. Providing minimal but relevant background information enables the AI to interpret instructions more accurately. This does not mean supplying exhaustive context, but rather selecting contextual cues that shape interpretation—such as purpose, intended use or constraints. Contextual anchoring reduces the likelihood that the AI will rely on default assumptions that may not match the user's needs.

A further technique involves making quality criteria explicit. Humans often have implicit standards for what constitutes a 'good' response, but generative AI cannot access these standards unless they are communicated. Indicating preferences for tone, rigour, creativity, neutrality or evidence-based reasoning helps align output with expectations. This practice reflects the principle of outcome orientation discussed in Chap. 3 and translates it into a concrete instructional form.

Finally, effective instructional communication recognises that task-giving is rarely final. Initial instructions may produce partial alignment, revealing assumptions or interpretations that require adjustment. Skilled users respond by refining instructions rather than replacing them entirely. This iterative refinement transforms instructional communication from a one-off command into a guided process that progressively improves alignment.

Instructional communication thus serves as the entry point to effective AI interaction. It appears simple but demands communicative discipline. By clearly defining tasks, controlling scope, anchoring context and articulating quality criteria, users transform generative AI from a reactive text generator into a responsive assistant capable of meaningful task execution. This technique establishes the foundation for more exploratory, contextual and collaborative communication strategies in the sections that follow (Fig. 4.1).

Fig. 4.1 Instructional communication: elements of clear task-giving. This diagram presents the four essential elements of effective instructional communication with generative AI. At the centre is a clear task definition, which translates human intent into an interpretable communicative form. Four supporting elements radiate outward: (1) explicit task definition that clearly states the cognitive operation (explain versus analyse, compare versus synthesize), (2) scope control that specifies boundaries including length, depth and audience focus, (3) contextual anchoring that provides minimal relevant context about purpose and situational constraints and (4) quality criteria that make standards explicit regarding tone, rigor and evidence-based reasoning. The diagram emphasises that task-giving is rarely final and benefits from iterative refinement based on initial output

4.2   Exploratory Communication: Thinking with AI

Exploratory communication represents a shift from task execution to collaborative sense-making. In this mode, generative AI is not asked to deliver a predefined output but to participate in the exploration of ideas, questions, or problem spaces. Rather than instructing the system to produce a specific result, the user engages it as a cognitive partner, using dialogue to think through possibilities, examine assumptions and generate alternative perspectives. Exploratory communication is especially valuable in situations where goals are not yet fully defined or where creative and analytical thinking must evolve dynamically.

Unlike instructional communication, exploratory communication embraces openness and provisionality. Users may begin with incomplete thoughts, tentative questions, or loosely framed problems. The AI's role is not to 'solve' the problem immediately but to help structure it—by suggesting angles, articulating implicit assumptions, or proposing lines of inquiry. This mode of communication aligns closely with human brainstorming, reflective dialogue and exploratory reasoning, but it requires explicit framing to avoid drifting into unfocused or superficial output.

A defining feature of exploratory communication is the deliberate suspension of premature closure. When users frame requests in exploratory terms, they signal that the goal is understanding rather than immediate production. Phrasing that invites exploration—such as asking the AI to 'consider', 'explore', 'outline possibilities', or 'reflect on implications'—encourages the system to generate diverse perspectives rather than converging on a single answer. This helps users expand their cognitive space before committing to a particular direction.

Exploratory communication also relies heavily on iterative exchange. Each AI response becomes a prompt for further questioning, clarification or redirection. Users may challenge the AI's suggestions, request elaboration, or introduce new constraints as their thinking develops. This back-and-forth interaction allows the dialogue to evolve in parallel with the user's reasoning. The value of the AI lies not in delivering a final answer but in supporting the process of thinking itself.

However, effective exploratory communication requires active guidance. Without communicative steering, the AI may generate output that is broad but shallow, or creative but disconnected from the user's interests. Users must therefore provide periodic signals about relevance, depth and direction. These signals can take the form of evaluative feedback ('this is useful', 'this is too general'), reframing ('let's focus on this aspect') or constraint introduction ('consider this from a practical perspective'). Such guidance maintains coherence while preserving exploratory openness.

Exploratory communication also plays a significant role in learning and problem formulation. Students, researchers and professionals can use AI to articulate questions more clearly, uncover gaps in understanding or examine issues from unfamiliar viewpoints. In this sense, the AI functions as a mirror that reflects and reshapes the user's thinking. This reflective function is particularly powerful when users explicitly articulate uncertainty, inviting the AI to help clarify rather than conceal it.

At the same time, exploratory communication requires careful management of trust and authority. Because generative AI can produce persuasive language, users must remain aware that exploratory suggestions are not validated conclusions. Treating exploratory output as provisional rather than authoritative preserves critical judgment and prevents the uncritical adoption of speculative ideas. Exploratory communication is most effective when paired with evaluation, verification and domain knowledge.

In human–AI collaboration, exploratory communication complements instructional communication. While instructional communication focuses on accomplishing defined tasks, exploratory communication supports idea generation, conceptual development and reflective reasoning. Together, these modes enable users to engage generative AI not only as a tool for execution but as a partner in thinking. This technique sets the stage for more context-sensitive and constraint-aware communication strategies, which are examined in the next section (Fig. 4.2).

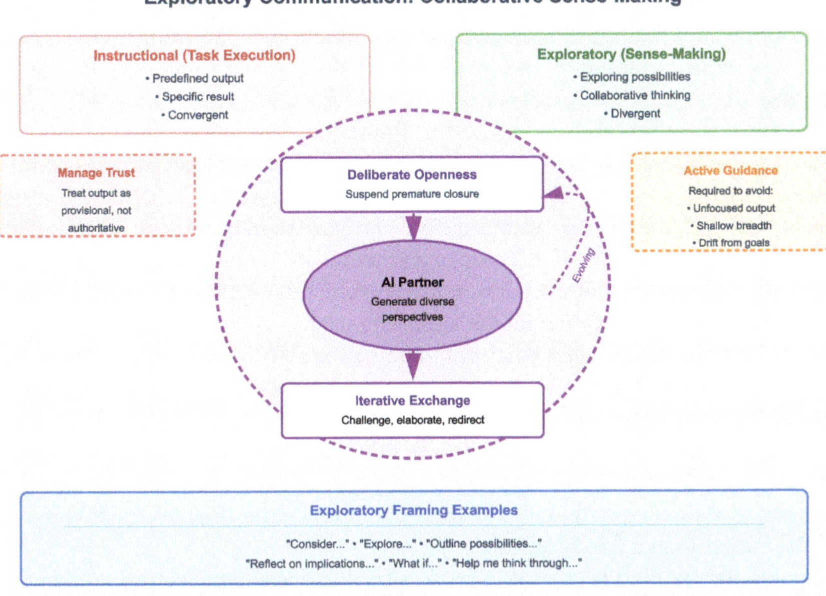

Fig. 4.2 Exploratory communication: collaborative sense-making. This diagram contrasts instructional task execution with exploratory sense-making and depicts the exploratory communication process as a cyclical partnership. Unlike instructional communication that seeks predefined outputs, exploratory communication embraces deliberate openness and suspends premature closure. The central process shows AI functioning as a thinking partner that generates diverse perspectives through iterative exchange, where users challenge, elaborate and redirect. Exploratory framing examples include phrases like 'consider', 'explore', 'outline possibilities' and 'reflect on implications.' The diagram includes cautions about the need for active guidance to avoid unfocused output and the importance of managing trust by treating exploratory suggestions as provisional rather than authoritative

4.3 Contextual Communication: Framing and Background

Contextual communication is the practice of deliberately framing tasks, questions and dialogue with relevant background information that enables generative AI to interpret user intent accurately. Because generative AI systems do not share human experience or situational awareness, they rely heavily on contextual cues embedded in communication. When context is absent or insufficient, the system defaults to generic assumptions, often producing output that is technically fluent but poorly aligned with the user's goals. Contextual communication addresses this limitation by shaping the interpretive environment in which AI operates.

Framing is the most immediate form of contextual communication. It establishes how the AI should understand the task at hand by indicating perspective, purpose and relevance. A framed request signals whether the user seeks explanation, evaluation, exploration or production and it clarifies the domain or situation in which the task is situated. Effective framing does not overwhelm the system with information; instead, it selects the cues that are most salient for interpretation. By framing requests explicitly, users reduce ambiguity and guide the AI toward more appropriate reasoning patterns.

Background information complements framing by supplying essential details that influence interpretation. This may include constraints, prior decisions, assumptions or situational factors that would otherwise remain implicit. In human communication, such information is often inferred through shared context. Generative AI lacks access to these shared references and therefore requires explicit articulation. Providing background information helps prevent misalignment caused by default assumptions embedded in the model's training data.

A key challenge in contextual communication lies in determining how much context to provide. Too little context leaves the AI guessing; too much context can dilute focus or introduce noise. Effective communicators learn to identify the minimal set of contextual elements that materially affect interpretation. This skill develops through experience and iteration, as users observe how changes in framing and background influence output. Contextual communication thus becomes a dynamic practice rather than a fixed formula.

Contextual framing is critical in professional and academic settings, where standards, conventions and constraints vary widely. A request that produces a satisfactory response in a casual context may be inadequate or inappropriate in a formal one. By communicating the intended audience, use case, or evaluative criteria, users enable the AI to adapt its tone, depth and structure accordingly. This alignment is essential for producing output that is not only correct but also usable.

Contextual communication also plays a critical role in managing continuity across dialogue. As interactions extend over multiple turns, the relevance of earlier context may fade unless it is reinforced. Skilled users monitor coherence and re-establish framing when necessary, particularly when shifting focus or introducing new objectives. This practice compensates for the AI's limited memory and supports sustained alignment over time.

Importantly, contextual communication supports ethical and responsible AI use. By explicitly stating constraints, sensitivities or normative boundaries, users can steer AI output away from problematic interpretations. Context helps the system understand not only what is possible but what is appropriate. In this way, contextual framing becomes a tool for aligning AI behaviour with human values and expectations.

Contextual communication bridges instructional and exploratory modes. It provides the grounding that allows tasks to be executed accurately and ideas to be explored meaningfully. By mastering framing and background provision, users transform generative AI from a generic responder into a context-aware collaborator. This technique prepares the ground for more structured constraint-based and iterative communication strategies, which are examined in the following sections (Fig. 4.3).

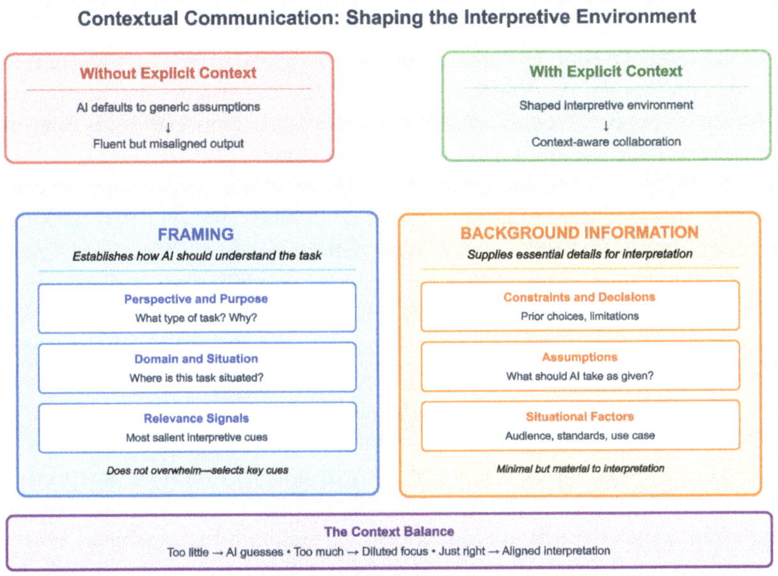

Fig. 4.3 Contextual communication: shaping the interpretive environment. This diagram compares communication outcomes with and without explicit context, then breaks down the two main components of contextual communication. Without context, AI defaults to generic assumptions, leading to fluent but misaligned output; with context, users create a shaped interpretive environment that enables context-aware collaboration. The left component presents framing, which establishes how AI should understand tasks through perspective and purpose, domain and situation and relevance signals—selecting key interpretive cues without overwhelming the system. The right component shows background information, which provides essential details, including constraints and decisions, assumptions and situational factors such as the audience and use case. The diagram emphasises finding the right balance: too little context causes AI to guess, too much dilutes focus, while the appropriate amount enables aligned interpretation

4.4 Constraint-Based Communication

Constraint-based communication is a technique in which users deliberately shape AI output by specifying boundaries within which generation occurs. Rather than directing the system toward a single outcome, constraints define what is acceptable, relevant or permissible. This approach reflects a fundamental insight into how generative AI operates: models perform best not when given maximal freedom or maximal control, but when their generative capacity is guided by well-chosen limitations.

In human communication, constraints are often implicit. Shared norms, situational awareness and cultural expectations restrict what can reasonably be said or done. Generative AI lacks access to these implicit boundaries. Without explicit constraints, it may generate content that is technically plausible yet inappropriate in scope, tone or relevance. Constraint-based communication compensates for this absence by making boundaries explicit and operational.

Constraints can take many forms. They may relate to content (what topics to include or exclude), scope (depth, length or level of detail), perspective (theoretical, practical or critical), tone (formal, neutral or persuasive) or method (step-by-step reasoning, comparison or synthesis). Importantly, constraints are not instructions about what to generate but conditions that shape how generation unfolds. They narrow the interpretive space without dictating a specific path.

One of the most common errors in AI communication is overgeneralisation. When users provide broad requests without constraints, the AI often responds with safe, generic output that reflects dominant patterns in its training data. Constraint-based communication counters this tendency by signalling what distinguishes the current task from a generic one. For example, specifying that an explanation should avoid introductory material, or that a comparison should focus only on conceptual differences rather than historical background, immediately improves relevance.

Constraint-based communication also supports cognitive alignment. By articulating boundaries, users externalise assumptions that might otherwise remain implicit. This reduces the risk that the AI will apply criteria or perspectives that conflict with the user's intentions. Constraints function as anchors that stabilise interpretation across iterative dialogue, helping maintain focus as tasks evolve.

Another essential function of constraints is ethical and practical risk management. Generative AI systems may produce speculative, biased, or misleading content when operating under broad instructions. Explicit constraints—such as requiring uncertainty to be acknowledged, limiting claims to well-supported information, or excluding sensitive interpretations—help mitigate these risks. Constraint-based communication thus contributes to responsible AI use by embedding safeguards directly into dialogue.

It is also important to distinguish constraints from rigidity. Effective constraint-based communication does not attempt to anticipate every possible issue or control every detail. Over-constraining an interaction can stifle practical exploration and increase cognitive load for both the user and the system. The goal is to identify the constraints that matter most for the task at hand and to allow flexibility elsewhere. Skilled users learn to introduce constraints incrementally, refining them as needed through iteration.

Constraint-based communication interacts closely with other techniques discussed in this chapter. It enhances instructional communication by sharpening task definition, supports exploratory communication by providing productive boundaries and strengthens contextual communication by clarifying relevance and appropriateness. Together, these techniques enable users to guide generative AI with precision while preserving its creative and analytical strengths.

By framing communication in terms of constraints rather than commands, users adopt a communicative stance that is both strategic and adaptive. Constraint-based communication recognises the interpretive nature of generative AI and responds with a method that balances openness and control. This balance is essential for achieving reliable, meaningful and responsible outcomes in human–AI collaboration (Fig. 4.4).

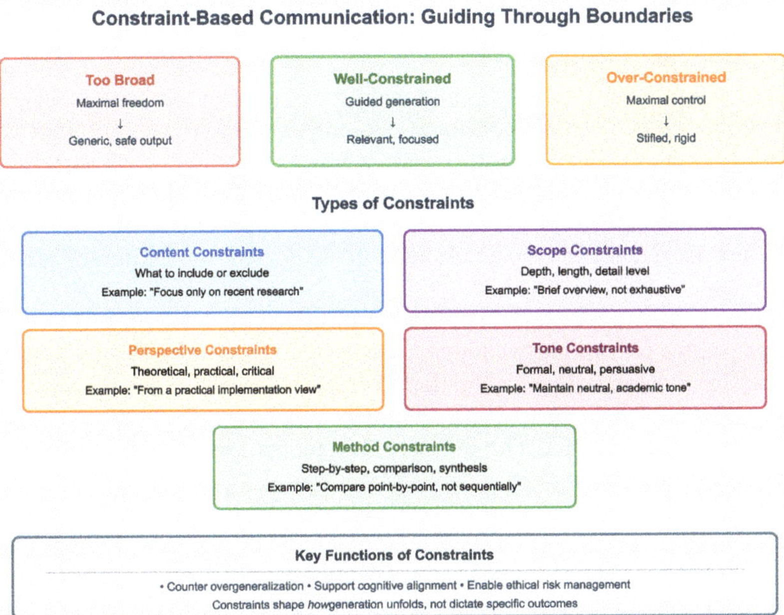

Fig. 4.4 Constraint-based communication: guiding through boundaries. This diagram maps the spectrum from too broad to well-constrained to over-constrained communication and categorises five types of constraints. The spectrum shows that maximal freedom produces generic output, well-chosen constraints yield relevant and focused results, while excessive constraints stifle exploration. Five constraint types are presented: content constraints (what to include/exclude), scope constraints (depth, length, detail level), perspective constraints (theoretical, practical, critical), tone constraints (formal, neutral, persuasive) and method constraints (step-by-step, comparison, synthesis). The diagram emphasises three key functions: countering overgeneralization, supporting cognitive alignment and enabling ethical risk management. Importantly, constraints shape how generation unfolds without dictating specific outcomes

4.5 Multi-step and Iterative Communication

Multi-step and iterative communication is a technique that explicitly recognises dialogue with generative AI as a process rather than a single exchange. Instead of attempting to encode all requirements into one comprehensive request, users decompose tasks into stages and guide the AI through a sequence of communicative steps. This approach reflects both the probabilistic nature of generative models and the limits of human foresight when formulating complex requests.

In traditional software interaction, tasks are often completed through a predefined workflow. Generative AI, however, does not follow fixed procedures unless they are articulated and reinforced through communication. Multi-step communication compensates for this by structuring dialogue incrementally. Users may begin by establishing goals, then request analysis, followed by refinement, evaluation or transformation. Each step builds on the previous one, allowing alignment to be checked and adjusted continuously.

A key advantage of multi-step communication is cognitive load management. Attempting to specify every constraint, assumption and outcome upfront can be cognitively demanding and error-prone. By contrast, breaking interaction into stages allows users to focus on one aspect of the task at a time. Early steps clarify direction; later steps increase precision. This staged approach mirrors effective human problem-solving practices and aligns naturally with the dialogical capabilities of generative AI.

Iteration is the mechanism that connects steps into a coherent process. After each AI response, the user evaluates alignment with intent and decides how to proceed. This may involve requesting elaboration, correcting misinterpretations, introducing new constraints or redirecting focus. Iteration transforms AI output into feedback rather than a final product. The dialogue becomes a shared workspace in which understanding and output evolve together.

Multi-step communication is particularly effective for complex analytical, creative or decision-support tasks. In such cases, the quality of the outcome depends not only on correct execution but on the gradual refinement of assumptions and priorities. By externalising this refinement through dialogue, users make their reasoning visible and adjustable. The AI, in turn, adapts its output to the evolving communicative context.

Importantly, multi-step communication also supports error detection and correction. Generative AI may introduce inaccuracies, inconsistencies or unintended interpretations at any stage. When interaction is structured as a sequence of steps, such issues are more likely to be identified early, before they propagate into later stages. This reduces the risk of compounding errors and supports responsible use in high-stakes contexts.

Another benefit of iterative dialogue is flexibility. Users may change direction as new insights emerge without needing to restart the interaction. Multi-step communication accommodates evolving goals by allowing re-framing at intermediate stages. This adaptability is particularly valuable in exploratory or creative work, where outcomes cannot be fully specified in advance.

It is important to note that multi-step communication does not require rigid planning. The number and nature of steps may vary depending on task complexity and user preference. What matters is recognising that alignment improves through progressive refinement rather than exhaustive initial specification. Skilled users learn to sense when a task requires further decomposition and when it has reached sufficient resolution.

Multi-step and iterative communication thus operationalises the principles of clarity, intent, iteration and cognitive alignment discussed in Chap. 3. It provides a practical method for managing complexity, uncertainty and variability in human–AI interaction. By embracing dialogue as a process, users transform generative AI from a one-shot responder into a participant in structured, evolving collaboration (Fig. 4.5).

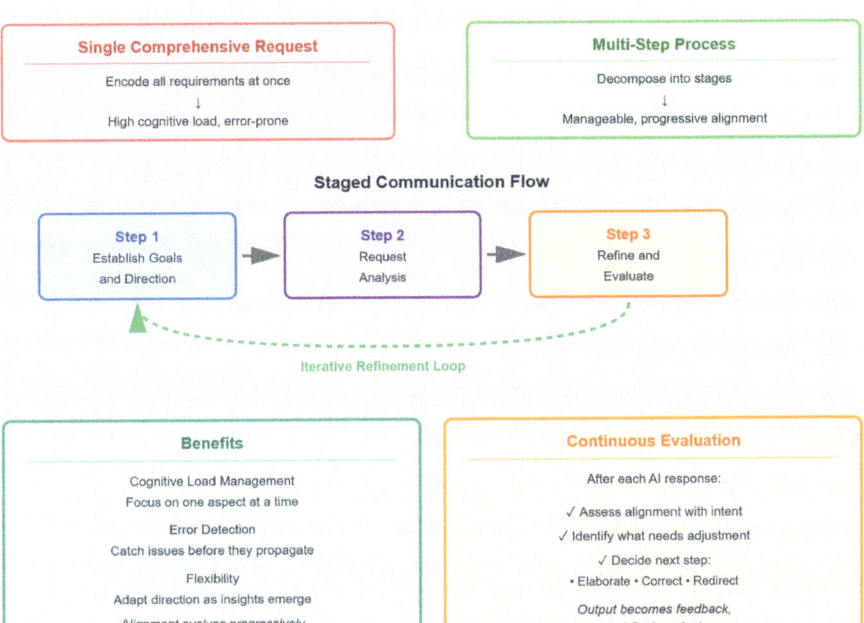

Fig. 4.5 Multi-step and iterative communication as process. This diagram contrasts single comprehensive requests with multi-step processes and visualises staged communication flow. Single comprehensive requests attempt to encode all requirements at once, creating high cognitive load and error-prone interactions. Multi-step processes decompose tasks into stages, enabling manageable and progressive alignment. The staged workflow shows three steps: establishing goals and direction, requesting analysis and refining and evaluating, connected by an iterative refinement loop. Benefits include cognitive load management (focusing on one aspect at a time), error detection (catching issues before they propagate) and flexibility (adapting direction as insights emerge). The diagram emphasises continuous evaluation, in which each AI response is assessed for alignment, with users deciding whether to elaborate, correct or redirect—treating the output as feedback rather than a final product

4.6 Tone, Style and Communication Persona

Tone and style are integral components of effective communication with generative AI. While they are often treated as aesthetic or secondary considerations, they play a significant role in shaping how AI systems interpret and generate responses. Generative models are highly sensitive to linguistic cues that signal formality, intent and relational stance. As a result, the tone and style adopted by the user influence not only the surface quality of the output but also its structure, depth and orientation.

Tone refers to the overall attitude conveyed through language—formal or informal, neutral or persuasive, exploratory or authoritative. Style encompasses choices related to structure, vocabulary, complexity and rhetorical form. In human–human communication, tone and style are negotiated dynamically and supported by shared social conventions. In human–AI communication, these cues must be made explicit through language itself. The AI infers expectations from how a request is framed and adapts its response accordingly.

Communication persona extends tone and style into a more sustained communicative stance. A persona reflects how the user positions themselves in relation to the AI and how they invite the AI to respond. For example, users may adopt a directive persona, focusing on task execution; a collaborative persona, engaging in joint reasoning; or an evaluative persona, emphasising critique and refinement. These stances shape the AI's output by signalling whether the interaction prioritises efficiency, exploration or judgement.

Explicitly managing tone and persona can significantly improve alignment. When users specify the desired tone—such as analytical, accessible, critical or creative—they reduce interpretive ambiguity and help the AI tailor its response to the intended context. This is particularly important in professional and academic settings, where mismatches in tone can undermine usability or credibility. Clear stylistic guidance ensures that output aligns with audience expectations and situational norms.

Tone and style also influence trust dynamics. Overly authoritative language may encourage users to accept AI output uncritically, while excessively casual tone may obscure limitations or reduce perceived reliability. Effective communicators calibrate tone to balance confidence and caution. By adopting a reflective and transparent persona, users reinforce their role as active evaluators rather than passive recipients of output.

Another important consideration is consistency. Maintaining a coherent tone and persona across multi-step interactions supports cognitive alignment and continuity. Abrupt shifts in tone or stance can confuse the AI's interpretive process, leading to inconsistent output. Skilled users monitor not only what they ask but how they ask it, adjusting tone deliberately when goals change.

Tone and style are also ethical levers. Polite, respectful communication reinforces norms of responsible use and reduces the likelihood of adversarial or manipulative interaction patterns. While generative AI does not experience respect in a human sense, communicative habits shape user expectations and behaviour. Treating AI interaction as a communicative practice rather than a mechanical operation fosters reflective engagement and supports ethical norms.

Finally, tone and persona interact closely with other techniques discussed in this chapter. Instructional clarity, exploratory openness, contextual framing and constraint-based guidance are all mediated through tone and style. Mastery of these elements enables users to communicate not only what they want but how they want to work with the AI.

By consciously managing tone, style and communication persona, users gain finer control over AI interaction while reinforcing their own agency. This technique underscores the book's central insight: effective communication with generative AI is not about issuing commands but about cultivating communicative awareness and

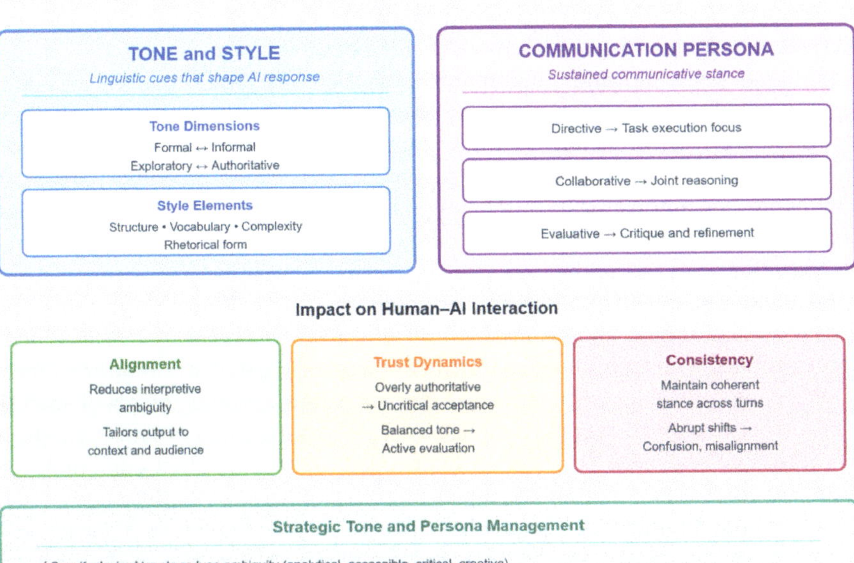

Fig. 4.6 Tone, style and communication persona. This diagram distinguishes between tone and style, on the one hand, and communication persona, on the other, and explores their impact on interaction. Tone and style are linguistic cues that shape AI responses along dimensions such as formal versus informal and exploratory versus authoritative, encompassing structure, vocabulary, complexity and rhetorical form. The communication persona represents a sustained communicative stance, with three types shown: directive (task-execution focus), collaborative (joint reasoning) and evaluative (critique and refinement). Three impact areas are identified: alignment (reducing interpretive ambiguity and tailoring output to context), trust dynamics (balancing confidence and caution to encourage active evaluation) and consistency (maintaining a coherent stance across turns to avoid confusion). Strategic considerations include specifying the desired tone, calibrating formality to audience expectations, monitoring consistency and using tone as an ethical lever to reinforce norms of responsible use

discipline. The final section of this chapter extends this insight into the multimodal domain, where communication expands beyond text alone (Fig. 4.6).

4.7 Multimodal Communication Strategies

Multimodal communication strategies extend human–AI interaction beyond text, enabling users to combine language with images, documents, diagrams, tables, audio and other input and output modalities. As generative AI systems increasingly support multimodal capabilities, effective communication requires users to develop skills for integrating and coordinating multiple modes of expression. Multimodality does not merely add convenience; it fundamentally changes how meaning is conveyed, interpreted and constructed in human–AI collaboration.

In human communication, multimodality is the norm rather than the exception. People routinely combine speech with gesture, text with images and explanation with demonstration. Generative AI now approximates this richness by interpreting and producing information across different modalities. However, unlike humans, AI systems do not automatically infer how modalities relate to one another. Multimodal communication, therefore, demands explicit guidance to ensure coherent interpretation.

A central principle of multimodal communication is intentional integration. When users provide multiple inputs—such as an image accompanied by text or a document combined with reaffirming instructions—they must indicate how these elements should be interpreted together. An image may serve as the primary object of analysis, a supporting example or a contextual reference. Without explicit clarification, the AI may misjudge relevance or focus on unintended aspects. Explicit communicative signalling ensures that multimodal inputs reinforce rather than confuse one another.

Multimodal strategies are particularly powerful for complex or abstract tasks. Visual inputs can convey spatial relationships, structural patterns or design intent that are difficult to describe verbally. Documents and tables provide dense contextual information that supports detailed analysis. Audio and conversational input enable more natural iterative dialogue. By combining modalities, users reduce cognitive friction and allow the AI to engage with problems in a more holistic manner.

At the same time, multimodal communication increases the importance of context management. Each modality introduces additional interpretive possibilities, which can amplify misalignment if not properly framed. Users must therefore articulate priorities: which modality carries primary meaning, which elements are illustrative and what outcomes are expected. This reinforces the broader communicative principles of clarity, intent and structure discussed earlier in the book.

Multimodal communication also supports iterative refinement. Users may begin with one modality to establish understanding and then introduce others to refine or extend the dialogue. For example, a textual description may be followed by an image to clarify intent, or an initial analysis may be refined through annotated documents. This layered approach aligns naturally with multi-step communication strategies and allows alignment to improve progressively.

Ethical considerations apply equally to multimodal interaction. Images, audio and documents may contain sensitive information, implicit biases, or contextual cues that influence interpretation. Responsible multimodal communication involves awareness of how different modalities shape meaning and how AI-generated multimodal output may be perceived or reused. Users must remain attentive to issues of representation, privacy and appropriate use when engaging across modalities.

Multimodal communication strategies also anticipate future developments in human–AI collaboration. As AI systems become more integrated into real-time environments—supporting speech, vision, gesture and persistent context—the ability to communicate fluently across modes will become a defining human competence.

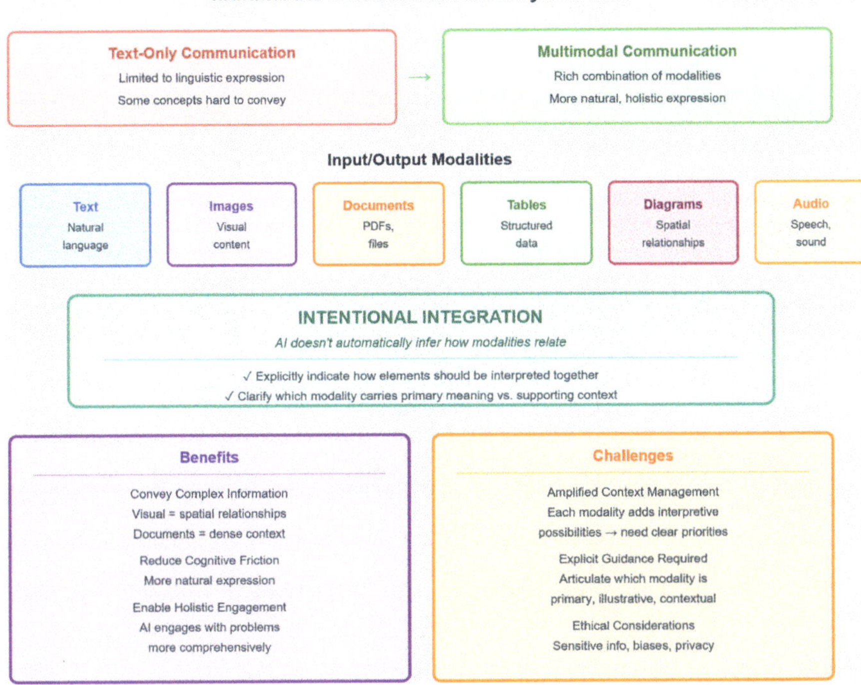

Fig. 4.7 Multimodal communication: beyond text. This diagram visualises the shift from text-only to multimodal communication and examines the benefits and challenges of integrating multiple modes. Six input/output modalities are shown: text (natural language), images (visual content), documents (PDFs and files), tables (structured data), diagrams (spatial relationships) and audio (speech and sound). The core principle of intentional integration emphasises that AI doesn't automatically infer how modalities relate—users must explicitly indicate relationships and clarify which modality carries primary meaning and which modality provides supporting context. Benefits include conveying complex information more naturally (visuals for spatial relationships, documents for dense context), reducing cognitive friction and enabling holistic engagement with problems. Challenges include amplified context-management needs, requirements for explicit guidance on modality priorities and ethical considerations regarding sensitive information, biases and privacy

Multimodal literacy will extend traditional communication skills into new domains, requiring adaptability and reflective practice.

In completing this chapter, multimodal communication highlights the unifying theme of effective AI interaction: communication is not about controlling output but about shaping meaning. Whether through text alone or through rich combinations of modalities, successful human–AI collaboration depends on intentional, reflective and ethically grounded communication practices. These techniques collectively prepare the reader for the challenges of misunderstanding, misalignment and trust explored in the next chapter (Fig. 4.7).

Bibliography

1. Brown, T.B., Mann, B., Ryder, et al.: Language Models are Few-Shot Learners. In: Advances in Neural Information Processing Systems, vol. 33, pp. 1877–1901. Curran Associates, Inc. (2020).
2. Codecademy: Learn Prompt Engineering Course. https://www.codecademy.com/learn/learn-prompt-engineering. Accessed 2 Nov 2024.
3. dair.ai: Prompt Engineering Guide. https://www.promptingguide.ai. Accessed 21 Nov 2024.
4. DeepLearning.AI: ChatGPT Prompt Engineering for Developers. https://www.deeplearning.ai/short-courses/chatgpt-prompt-engineering-for-developers/. Accessed 7 Oct 2024.
5. Eliot, L.: Essentials of Prompt Engineering for Generative AI: Practical Advances in Artificial Intelligence and Machine Learning. LBE Press Publishing (2024).
6. Fu, Y., Peng, H., Sabharwal, A., Clark, P., Khot, T.: Complexity-Based Prompting for Multi-Step Reasoning. arXiv preprint arXiv:2210.00720 (2022).
7. Garg, S., Tsipras, D., Liang, P., Valiant, G.: What Can Transformers Learn In-Context? A Case Study of Simple Function Classes. arXiv preprint arXiv:2208.01066 (2022).
8. Geroimenko, V.: The Essential Guide to Prompt Engineering: Key Principles, Techniques, Challenges, and Security Risks, Springer, Cham (2025)
9. Geroimenko, V.: Beyond and After Prompt Engineering: The Future of AI Communication, Springer, Cham (2026)
10. Geroimenko, V. (ed.): Human-Computer Creativity: Generative AI in Education, Art, and Healthcare, Springer, Cham (2025)
11. GitHub: Prompt Engineering Repository. https://github.com/NirDiamant/Prompt_Engineering. Accessed 25 Oct 2024.
12. Hunter, N.: The Art of Prompt Engineering with ChatGPT: A Hands-on Guide. AI Press (2023).
13. Jung, J., Qin, L., Welleck, S., Brahman, F., Bhagavatula, C.: Maieutic Prompting: Logically Consistent Reasoning with Recursive Explanations. arXiv preprint arXiv:2304.09842 (2023).
14. Kansal, A.: Prompt Engineering Techniques. In: Building Generative AI-Powered Apps. Apress, Berkeley, CA (2024). https://doi.org/10.1007/979-8-8688-0205-8_8
15. Khan, I.: The Quick Guide to Prompt Engineering. Wiley (2024).
16. Kojima, T., Gu, S.S., Reid, M., Matsuo, Y., Iwasawa, Y.: Large Language Models are Zero-Shot Reasoners. arXiv preprint arXiv:2205.11916 (2022).
17. LambdaTest: Prompt Engineering Tutorial. https://www.lambdatest.com/learning-hub/prompt-engineering. Accessed 3 Nov 2024.
18. Learn Prompting: https://learnprompting.org. Accessed 15 Oct 2024.
19. Li, Z., Peng, B., He, P., Galley, M., Gao, J.: Guiding Large Language Models via Directional Stimulus Prompting. arXiv preprint arXiv:2305.12345 (2023).
20. Liu, J., Liu, A., Lu, X., Welleck, S., West, P.: Generated Knowledge Prompting for Commonsense Reasoning. In: Proceedings of the 60th Annual Meeting of the Association for Computational Linguistics (Volume 1: Long Papers), pp. 3154–3169. Association for Computational Linguistics (2022).
21. Madaan, A., Tandon, N., Gupta, P., Hallinan, S., Gao, L., Callison-Burch, C.: Self-Refine: Iterative Refinement with Self-Feedback. arXiv preprint arXiv:2303.17651 (2023).
22. Marvin, G., Hellen, N., Jjingo, D., Nakatumba-Nabende, J.: Prompt Engineering in Large Language Models. In: Jacob, I.J., Piramuthu, S., Falkowski-Gilski, P. (eds) Data Intelligence and Cognitive Informatics. ICDICI 2023. Algorithms for Intelligent Systems. Springer, Singapore (2024) https://doi.org/10.1007/978-981-99-7962-2_30
23. McTear, M., Ashurkina, M.: Advanced Prompt Engineering. In: Transforming Conversational AI. Apress, Berkeley, CA (2024). https://doi.org/10.1007/979-8-8688-0110-5_6
24. OpenAI Help Center: Best Practices for Prompt Engineering with the OpenAI API. https://help.openai.com/en/articles/6654000-best-practices-for-prompt-engineering-with-the-openai-api. Accessed 17 Oct 2024.
25. OpenAI: Prompt Engineering Documentation. https://platform.openai.com/docs/guides/prompt-engineering. Accessed 18 Oct 2024.

26. Ouyang, L., Wu, J., Jiang, X., Almeida, D., et al.: Training Language Models to Follow Instructions with Human Feedback. arXiv preprint arXiv:2203.02155 (2022).
27. Phoenix, J., Taylor, M.: Prompt Engineering for Generative AI. O'Reilly Media (2024).
28. Sahoo, P., Singh, A.K., Saha, S., Jain, V., Mondal, S., Chadha, A.: A Systematic Survey of Prompt Engineering in Large Language Models: Techniques and Applications. arXiv preprint arXiv:2402.07927 (2024).
29. Schulhoff, S., et al.: The Prompt Report: A Systematic Survey of Prompting Techniques. arXiv preprint arXiv:2406.06608 (2024).
30. Sibal, A.: Hands-On Prompt Engineering: Learning to Program ChatGPT Using OpenAI APIs. Wiley (2025).
31. Singh, B.: Magic of Prompt Engineering. In: Building Applications with Large Language Models. Apress, Berkeley, CA (2024). https://doi.org/10.1007/979-8-8688-0569-1_4
32. Soh, J., Singh, P.: Prompt Engineering Techniques, Small Language Models, and Fine-Tuning. In: Data Science Solutions on Azure. Apress, Berkeley, CA (2024). https://doi.org/10.1007/979-8-8688-0914-9_6
33. Unite.AI: Prompt Engineering Courses. https://www.unite.ai/prompt-engineering-courses/. Accessed 2 Nov 2024.
34. Vairamani, A.D., Nayyar, A.: Prompt Engineering: Empowering Communication. CRC Press (2024).
35. Wang, X., Wei, J., Schuurmans, D., Le, Q., Chi, E., Zhou, D.: Self-Consistency Improves Chain of Thought Reasoning in Language Models. arXiv preprint arXiv:2203.11171 (2022).
36. Wei, J., Wang, X., Schuurmans, D., Bosma, M., et al.: Chain of Thought Prompting Elicits Reasoning in Large Language Models. arXiv preprint arXiv:2201.11903 (2022).
37. Yao, S., Yu, D., Zhao, J., Shafran, I., et al.: Tree of Thoughts: Deliberate Problem Solving with Large Language Models. arXiv preprint arXiv:2305.10601 (2023).
38. Zhang, T., Roller, S., Goyal, N., et al.: OPT: Open Pre-trained Transformer Language Models. arXiv preprint arXiv:2205.01068 (2022).
39. Zhou, D., Schärli, N., Hou, L., Wei, et al.: Least-to-Most Prompting Enables Complex Reasoning in Large Language Models. arXiv preprint arXiv:2205.10625 (2022).

Chapter 5
Communication Pitfalls, Errors and Misunderstandings

Effective communication with generative AI is not guaranteed by good intentions or technical familiarity alone. Even skilled and experienced users frequently encounter misunderstandings, misalignment and unexpected behaviour. This chapter focuses on why such failures occur and how they can be understood as communicative phenomena rather than isolated system flaws. By analysing common user errors, interpretive limitations of generative models and the psychological dynamics of trust and expectation, the chapter provides a diagnostic lens for identifying breakdowns in human–AI dialogue. It also examines how safety mechanisms and refusals influence communication and user response. Understanding these pitfalls is essential for developing mature AI communication literacy and prepares the reader for the collaborative and co-creative communication practices explored in the next chapter.

5.1 Common User Errors and How to Avoid Them

Many communication failures in human–AI interaction arise not from technical shortcomings of generative AI systems but from systematic user errors. These errors reflect mismatches between human communicative habits—shaped by human–human interaction and traditional software use—and the interpretive characteristics of generative models. Understanding these common pitfalls is essential for developing robust AI communication skills and for avoiding predictable misunderstandings.

One of the most prevalent user errors is under-specification. Users often assume that minimal input is sufficient for the AI to infer their intentions, relying on implicit context or shared understanding that does not exist. This leads to vague requests that produce generic or misaligned responses. Under-specification is particularly common among experienced professionals who are accustomed to working with human collaborators who can fill in gaps. With generative AI, however, missing

© The Author(s), under exclusive license to Springer Nature Switzerland AG 2026

V. Geroimenko, *Communication Skills for Generative AI*, Human–Computer Interaction Series, https://doi.org/10.1007/978-3-032-21689-2_5

context is not compensated for by intuition but by probabilistic inference, which may diverge significantly from the user's intent. Avoiding this error requires deliberate articulation of goals, constraints and expectations.

A closely related error is over-generalisation. Users may frame requests so broadly that the AI has no clear basis for prioritisation. In response, the system defaults to conventional or widely represented patterns, often producing safe but unremarkable output. Over-generalisation is frequently mistaken for an AI limitation, when in fact it reflects insufficient communicative guidance. The remedy lies in strategic narrowing—introducing scope, focus, or evaluative criteria that distinguish the task from a generic request.

Another common mistake is treating AI output as authoritative. Generative AI systems produce fluent, confident language, which can lead users to overestimate their reliability. This error is particularly dangerous in academic, professional and decision-making contexts. Users may accept outputs without verification, conflating coherence with correctness. Avoiding this pitfall requires maintaining an evaluative stance and recognising that AI output represents inferred plausibility rather than validated truth. Communicative practices that encourage transparency—such as requesting reasoning or acknowledging uncertainty—help mitigate this risk.

Users also frequently underestimate the importance of iteration. Expecting a single request to produce a fully aligned result, they may discard AI output prematurely or attribute misalignment to system failure. This transactional mindset overlooks the dialogical nature of generative AI communication. Misinterpretation often reflects incomplete alignment rather than incapacity. Iterative refinement—clarifying intent, adjusting constraints and responding to AI output—transforms initial misalignment into productive collaboration.

Another error involves inconsistent or shifting communicative signals. Users may change goals, tone or expectations without explicitly communicating these changes. From the AI's perspective, such shifts appear arbitrary, weakening coherence across dialogue turns. Effective communication requires signalling transitions explicitly, especially in multi-step interactions. Consistency does not imply rigidity, but it does require awareness of how changes in communicative stance affect interpretation.

Finally, many users import inappropriate mental models from earlier technologies. Treating AI as a search engine, a human expert or a deterministic tool leads to mismatched expectations and communicative strategies. These models shape how users phrase requests, interpret responses and assign responsibility. Correcting these mental models—by understanding AI as an interpretive, probabilistic system—reduces error frequency and improves alignment.

Importantly, these user errors are not signs of incompetence. They reflect the novelty of human–AI communication and the absence of established norms. By identifying common pitfalls and adopting reflective communication practices, users can significantly improve interaction quality. Avoiding these errors is not about mastering technical tricks, but about cultivating communicative awareness, discipline and responsibility—skills that form the core of effective AI communication literacy (Fig. 5.1).

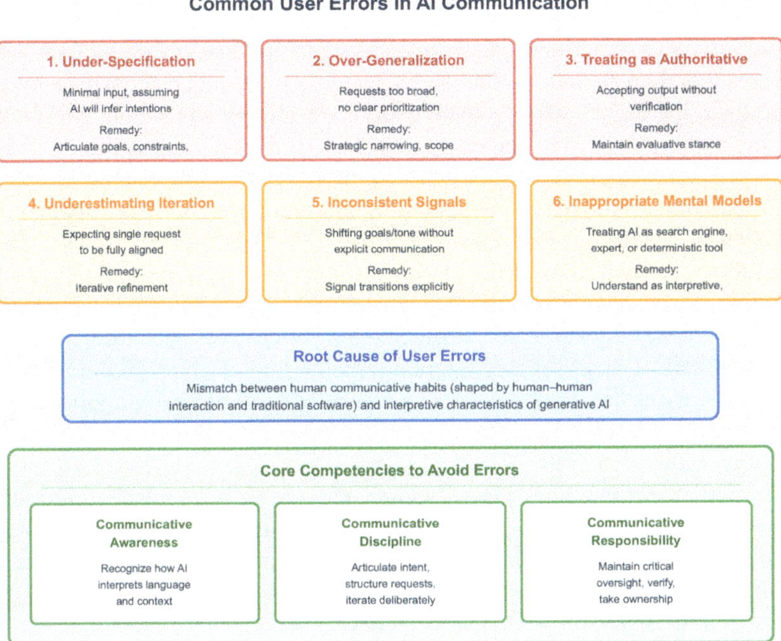

Fig. 5.1 Common user errors in AI communication. This diagram identifies six systematic user errors that arise from mismatches between human communicative habits and the interpretive characteristics of generative AI. The errors include: (1) under-specification where minimal input assumes AI will infer intentions, remedied by articulating goals and constraints; (2) over-generalisation with requests too broad for clear prioritisation, addressed through strategic narrowing; (3) treating output as authoritative by accepting without verification, corrected by maintaining an evaluative stance; (4) underestimating iteration by expecting single requests to be fully aligned, resolved through iterative refinement; (5) inconsistent signals where goals or tone shift without explicit communication, fixed by signalling transitions explicitly; and (6) inappropriate mental models that treat AI as a search engine or deterministic tool, remedied by understanding AI as an interpretive, probabilistic system. The diagram emphasises that these errors reflect the novelty of human–AI communication rather than user incompetence and that they require the development of three core competencies: communicative awareness, discipline and responsibility

5.2 Model Misinterpretations and Hallucinations

Model misinterpretations and hallucinations are among the most widely discussed—and most misunderstood—sources of error in generative AI communication. These phenomena are often framed as technical failures of the system. While they do reflect limitations of current AI architectures, they are equally shaped by the communicative context in which AI operates. Understanding why misinterpretations and hallucinations occur and how communication practices influence them, is essential for effective and responsible human–AI interaction.

A model misinterpretation occurs when the AI infers an intent, scope or constraint different from what the user intended. Because generative AI systems rely on probabilistic inference rather than semantic understanding, they interpret input based on patterns rather than meaning. When input is ambiguous, underspecified or internally inconsistent, the model resolves uncertainty by selecting a plausible interpretation. From the user's perspective, the response may appear irrelevant or misguided, even though it is coherent within the model's inferred frame. Misinterpretation is therefore not random error but a predictable outcome of interpretive inference under uncertainty.

Hallucinations are a more specific manifestation of this process. They occur when the model generates information that is fluent and plausible but factually incorrect, unverifiable or entirely fabricated. Hallucinations often arise when the model is asked to supply details it lacks reliable internal patterns for—such as obscure facts, non-existent references or speculative claims presented as definitive. Importantly, hallucinations are not deliberate deceptions. They reflect the model's optimisation for plausibility rather than truth.

Communication practices play a significant role in both misinterpretation and hallucination. Broad or confident-sounding requests may signal to the AI that a definitive answer is expected, even when uncertainty is appropriate. Similarly, requests that implicitly assume the existence of information—such as asking for precise details without establishing whether such details are known—encourage the model to generate content rather than acknowledge limits. In this sense, hallucinations are often co-produced by communicative framing.

Effective AI communication mitigates these risks through explicit uncertainty management. Users can reduce hallucination by signalling tolerance for uncertainty, requesting conditional responses or asking the AI to distinguish between known information and inference. Transparency-oriented communication—such as requesting reasoning, assumptions or confidence levels—also helps users detect when output may be speculative. These practices align with the broader principle of cognitive alignment discussed earlier in the book.

Another critical factor is the cumulative effect of dialogue. Once a misinterpretation enters the conversational context, subsequent responses may build upon it, amplifying the error. This compounding effect is especially pronounced in multi-step interactions where early assumptions are not corrected. Skilled communicators actively monitor for divergence and intervene early by correcting or reframing. Iterative communication thus serves as a corrective mechanism, preventing minor misalignments from escalating into significant inaccuracies.

It is also crucial to distinguish between hallucination and creative extrapolation. In exploratory or creative contexts, generating novel or speculative ideas may be desirable. Problems arise when such output is mistaken for factual or authoritative information. Clear communication about the intended mode—exploratory versus factual—helps align expectations and evaluation standards.

Ultimately, misinterpretations and hallucinations highlight the interpretive limits of generative AI and the central role of human oversight. They reinforce the need for communicative discipline rather than blind trust. By understanding these phenomena as interactional outcomes rather than isolated technical defects, users can adopt communication strategies that reduce risk, improve reliability and support responsible AI use (Fig. 5.2).

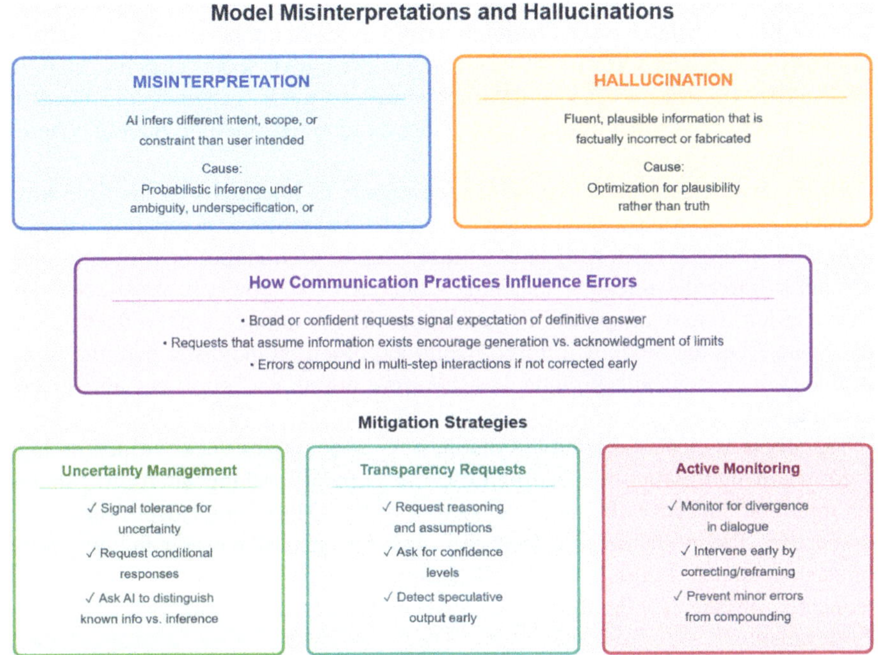

Fig. 5.2 Model misinterpretations and hallucinations. This diagram distinguishes between two related but distinct types of AI errors and their mitigation strategies. Misinterpretation occurs when AI infers a different intent, scope, or constraint than intended, caused by probabilistic inference under ambiguity or under-specification. Hallucination involves fluent, plausible information that is factually incorrect or fabricated, resulting from optimisation for plausibility rather than truth. Communication practices significantly influence both: broad or confident requests signal an expectation of definitive answers even when uncertainty is appropriate, requests that assume information exists encourage generation over acknowledgement of limits, and errors compound in multi-step interactions if uncorrected. Three mitigation strategies are presented: uncertainty management (signalling tolerance for uncertainty, requesting conditional responses, asking AI to distinguish known information from inference), transparency requests (asking for reasoning, assumptions and confidence levels to detect speculative output) and active monitoring (watching for divergence in dialogue, intervening early through correction or reframing to prevent compounding errors)

5.3 Ambiguity, Vagueness and Implicit Assumptions

Ambiguity, vagueness and implicit assumptions are among the most persistent sources of misunderstanding in human–AI communication. Unlike overt user errors or obvious system failures, these issues often go unnoticed because they are deeply embedded in everyday human communicative habits. In human–human interaction, ambiguity is frequently resolved through shared context, social cues and iterative clarification. Generative AI systems lack access to these resources and therefore interpret ambiguous input through probabilistic inference, often producing coherent but misaligned responses.

Ambiguity arises when a request can reasonably be interpreted in multiple ways. This may involve unclear task definitions, undefined terms or competing priorities within the same instruction. Humans often tolerate such ambiguity, trusting interlocutors to infer the intended meaning. Generative AI, however, must select one interpretation from many plausible alternatives. The resulting output reflects not the user's intent but the model's inferred likelihood based on linguistic patterns. When ambiguity is present, misalignment is therefore not an exception but an expected outcome.

Vagueness is closely related but distinct. A vague request lacks sufficient detail to constrain interpretation meaningfully. For example, asking an AI to 'analyse this topic' or 'improve this text' provides little guidance about depth, criteria or perspective. The model defaults to generic conventions, often producing output that appears reasonable but fails to meet the user's unstated expectations. Vagueness is frequently mistaken for flexibility, but in AI communication, it usually leads to a loss of relevance.

Implicit assumptions further complicate communication. Users routinely assume that certain information, standards or constraints are obvious and need not be stated. These assumptions may relate to domain knowledge, audience, ethical boundaries or intended use. In human communication, such assumptions are often valid because they are grounded in shared experience. In human–AI communication, they are invisible unless explicitly articulated. The AI cannot access what the user assumes; it can only infer from what is communicated.

These issues are particularly problematic because they interact. A vague request may contain implicit assumptions and ambiguous phrasing may conceal conflicting expectations. The AI resolves these uncertainties by generating output that aligns with dominant patterns in its training data rather than with the user's specific context. This can result in responses that are fluent, confident and superficially appropriate, yet still fail to satisfy the user's needs.

Addressing ambiguity and vagueness requires a shift from implicit to explicit communication. Users must learn to externalise assumptions that would otherwise remain unstated. This includes clarifying terms, specifying criteria and indicating priorities. Explicitness does not imply verbosity; it involves identifying which aspects of a request are critical for interpretation. Communicative discipline, rather than exhaustive detail, is the key to reducing ambiguity.

Iterative dialogue also plays an essential corrective role. Initial AI responses often reveal how a request has been interpreted. Users who recognise misalignment can then clarify or reframe, gradually converging on shared understanding. Treating early responses as diagnostic rather than final reduces frustration and improves outcomes.

Importantly, not all ambiguity is undesirable. In exploratory or creative contexts, ambiguity may serve as a productive space for idea generation. Problems arise when ambiguity is unintended or when exploratory output is evaluated using factual or decision-oriented criteria. Explicit signalling of communicative intent—whether exploratory, analytical or decisive—helps align interpretation and evaluation.

By recognising ambiguity, vagueness and implicit assumptions as central challenges rather than minor flaws, users can develop more robust communication practices. Addressing these issues strengthens alignment, reduces error and reinforces the human's role as an active participant in meaning-making. These challenges also highlight why effective AI communication is a learned skill rather than an intuitive extension of existing digital literacy (Fig. 5.3).

5.4 Overtrust and Undertrust in AI Responses

Trust plays a central role in human–AI communication, shaping how users interpret, evaluate and act upon AI-generated output. Miscalibrated trust—either excessive or insufficient—represents a significant source of communication failure. Overtrust and undertrust are not independent errors to avoid; they are two manifestations of the same underlying challenge: the difficulty of forming accurate mental models of generative AI's capabilities and limitations.

Overtrust occurs when users attribute greater reliability, understanding or authority to AI systems than is warranted. Generative AI produces fluent, confident and well-structured language, creating a powerful illusion of competence. Users may therefore accept output uncritically, assuming correctness where only plausibility is guaranteed. This risk is particularly acute in domains that value articulate reasoning—such as academia, policy, law or medicine—where linguistic confidence is often associated with expertise.

Overtrust is often reinforced by successful early interactions. When AI performs well on familiar or low-risk tasks, users may generalise that success to more complex or high-stakes situations without adjusting their evaluative stance. Communicatively, this manifests as reduced scrutiny, fewer clarification requests and diminished verification. The AI becomes perceived as an authority rather than a tool or partner, undermining human agency and responsibility.

Undertrust, by contrast, arises when users underestimate AI capability or treat it as inherently unreliable. This may result from awareness of hallucinations, public discourse emphasising AI failure, or prior negative experiences. Users who undertrust AI tend to restrict interaction to trivial tasks or to disregard potentially valuable insights. Communicatively, undertrust leads to shallow engagement and missed opportunities for productive collaboration.

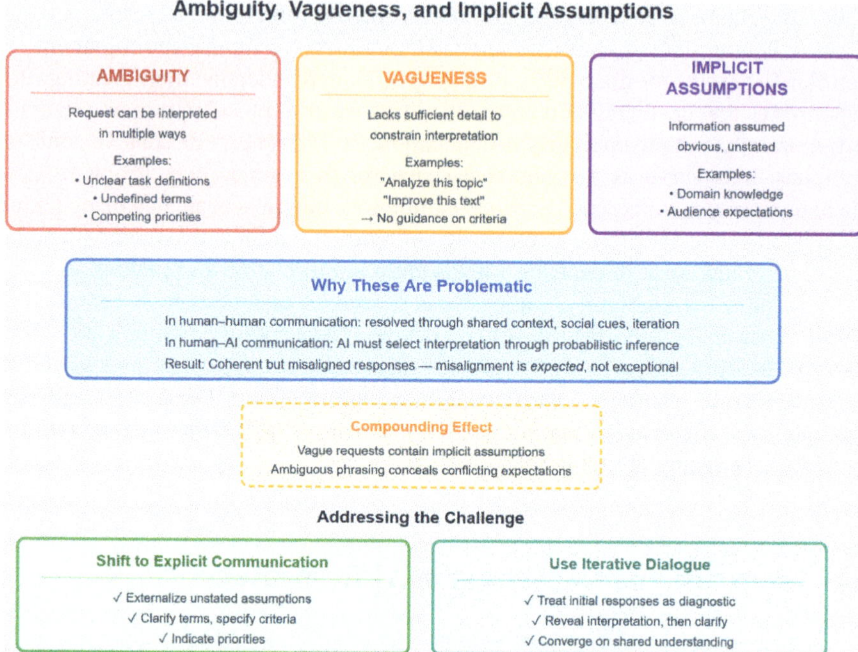

Fig. 5.3 Ambiguity, vagueness and implicit assumptions. This diagram analyses three persistent sources of misunderstanding in human–AI communication that are deeply embedded in everyday human communicative habits. Ambiguity arises when requests can be interpreted in multiple ways through unclear task definitions, undefined terms or competing priorities. Vagueness occurs when requests lack sufficient detail to constrain interpretation, as in 'analyse this topic' or 'improve this text' without guidance on criteria. Implicit assumptions involve information users consider obvious but leave unstated, including domain knowledge and audience expectations. The diagram explains why these are problematic: while human–human communication resolves such issues through shared context and social cues, AI must select interpretations through probabilistic inference, making coherent but misaligned responses expected rather than exceptional. These issues compound when vague requests contain implicit assumptions and ambiguous phrasing conceals conflicting expectations. Two solutions are presented: shifting to explicit communication by externalising assumptions, clarifying terms and indicating priorities; and using iterative dialogue by treating initial responses as diagnostic, revealing interpretation before clarifying to converge on shared understanding

Both overtrust and undertrust are shaped by communication practices. Overtrust is reinforced when users frame requests in ways that implicitly demand certainty or finality, whereas undertrust is reinforced when interactions remain superficial and transactional. In both cases, miscalibration reduces the quality and effectiveness of communication.

Calibrated trust requires active communicative management. Users must adopt an evaluative stance that treats AI output as provisional and context-dependent. This involves requesting transparency, asking for reasoning and cross-checking essential claims. It also involves recognising domains where AI excels—such as synthesis, pattern exploration and language generation—and those where it is less reliable, such as factual precision without verification.

Iterative communication supports trust calibration by revealing how the AI responds as it refines. When users engage in dialogue rather than one-shot interaction, they gain insight into the system's interpretive behaviour and limitations. This experiential understanding supports more accurate mental models and more nuanced trust.

Trust is also influenced by emotional and cognitive factors. AI can reduce cognitive effort, increase productivity and provide a sense of support, which may encourage reliance. At the same time, awareness of AI fallibility can generate anxiety or scepticism. Effective communication practices help regulate these responses by embedding reflection and verification into interaction.

Importantly, calibrated trust does not imply neutrality or detachment. It enables confident use of AI while preserving critical oversight. Users who calibrate trust effectively are neither dependent nor dismissive. They communicate with AI as a capable but limited partner, integrating its contributions into human judgement rather than replacing it.

Understanding overtrust and undertrust as communicative challenges underscores the ethical dimension of AI interaction. Responsible use requires not only technical safeguards but also communicative awareness. By cultivating calibrated trust through transparent, iterative and reflective dialogue, users can avoid both blind reliance and unnecessary rejection, supporting effective and responsible human–AI collaboration (Fig. 5.4).

5.5 Guardrails, Refusals and Safety Boundaries

Guardrails, refusals and safety boundaries are integral features of contemporary generative AI systems. They are designed to prevent harmful use, reduce legal and ethical risk and align AI behaviour with societal norms. From a communication perspective, however, these mechanisms also introduce a distinct class of misunderstandings. Users may interpret refusals as system failure, censorship, or incompetence, when in fact they are often the result of misaligned communication or boundary conditions embedded in the system's design.

Guardrails operate by constraining what the AI can generate in response to specific inputs. These constraints may relate to safety, legality, ethics, or policy compliance. Importantly, they do not function as explicit rules that are visible to the user. Instead, they are triggered probabilistically based on how requests are framed and interpreted. As a result, similar requests phrased differently may receive different responses, including partial answers, redirections or outright refusals. This variability can be confusing for users who expect consistent behaviour.

A typical communication pitfall arises when users interpret refusals as absolute limitations rather than context-sensitive outcomes. In many cases, a refusal does

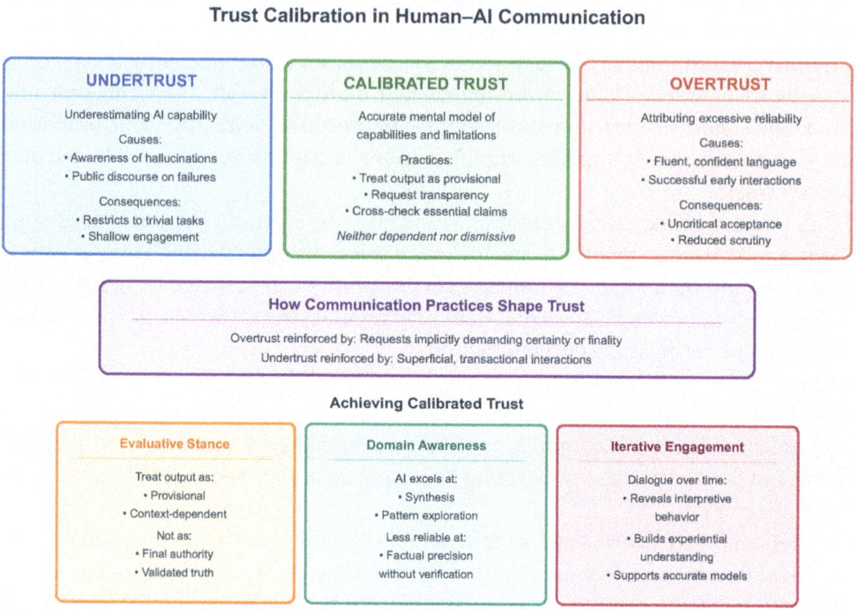

Trust Calibration in Human–AI Communication

Fig. 5.4 Trust calibration in human–AI communication. This diagram maps the trust spectrum from undertrust through calibrated trust to overtrust, examining how communication practices shape trust dynamics. Undertrust involves underestimating AI capabilities due to awareness of hallucinations or public discourse about failures, resulting in a restriction to trivial tasks and shallow engagement. Overtrust involves attributing excessive reliability due to fluent, confident language and successful early interactions, leading to uncritical acceptance and reduced scrutiny. Calibrated trust represents accurate mental models of capabilities and limitations, characterised by treating output as provisional, requesting transparency and cross-checking essential claims—being neither dependent nor dismissive. The diagram shows how communication practices shape trust: overtrust is reinforced by requests implicitly demanding certainty or finality, while undertrust is reinforced by superficial, transactional interactions. Three paths to calibration are detailed: adopting an evaluative stance that treats output as provisional and context-dependent rather than final authority; developing domain awareness of where AI excels (synthesis, pattern exploration) versus where it's less reliable (factual precision without verification); and engaging iteratively over time to reveal interpretive behaviour, build experiential understanding and support accurate mental models

not indicate that the task itself is forbidden, but that the way it was framed triggered a safety boundary. Users may respond by abandoning the task altogether or by attempting adversarial reformulations. Both reactions reflect misunderstanding. Effective communication involves recognising refusals as signals that alignment has failed and that reframing may be necessary.

Refusals also highlight the importance of intent signalling. Generative AI systems attempt to infer not only what is being asked, but why it is being asked. Requests that lack contextual grounding or appear ambiguous in intent may be interpreted conservatively. By clearly articulating legitimate purpose, scope and constraints, users can often avoid unnecessary refusals and obtain appropriate assistance within system boundaries. This reinforces the broader principle that clarity and context are not merely helpful but essential.

Safety boundaries also interact with trust and agency. Users who encounter unexpected refusals may lose confidence in the system or perceive it as obstructive. Conversely, users who attempt to bypass guardrails may undermine responsible use and reinforce adversarial interaction patterns. Communicative maturity involves accepting that safety constraints are part of the interaction landscape and learning to work productively within them.

From an ethical perspective, guardrails serve an important protective function, but they also shift some responsibility onto the user. Because boundaries are not always transparent, users must remain attentive to how their requests are framed and how the system responds. Ethical AI communication involves respecting safety constraints rather than treating them as obstacles to be overcome. This stance supports trust, accountability and sustainable use.

It is also essential to recognise that safety mechanisms are evolving. As generative AI systems are deployed across diverse cultural, legal and professional contexts, guardrails will continue to adapt. Users who develop flexible communication skills—such as reframing, contextual clarification and outcome-oriented dialogue—are better equipped to navigate these changes without frustration or misuse.

Ultimately, guardrails and refusals are not external interruptions to communication but part of the communicative environment itself. They shape what can be said, how it can be said and under what conditions assistance is provided. Understanding them as communicative signals rather than arbitrary constraints enables users to respond constructively. By integrating awareness of safety boundaries into their communication practices, users reinforce responsible, effective and ethically grounded human–AI collaboration (Fig. 5.5).

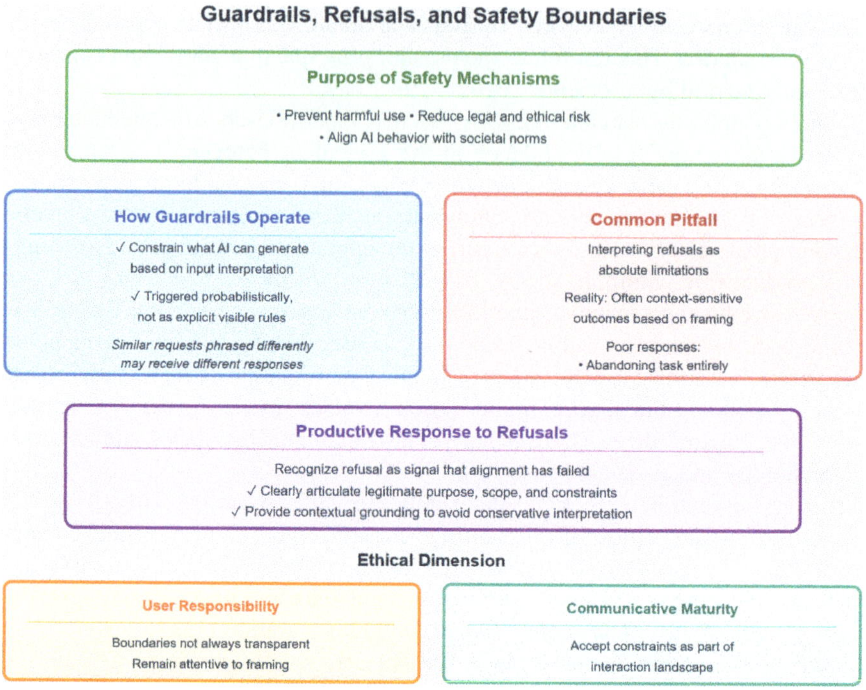

Guardrails, Refusals, and Safety Boundaries

Purpose of Safety Mechanisms

• Prevent harmful use • Reduce legal and ethical risk
• Align AI behavior with societal norms

How Guardrails Operate

✓ Constrain what AI can generate
based on input interpretation

✓ Triggered probabilistically,
not as explicit visible rules

*Similar requests phrased differently
may receive different responses*

Common Pitfall

Interpreting refusals as
absolute limitations

Reality: Often context-sensitive
outcomes based on framing

Poor responses:
• Abandoning task entirely

Productive Response to Refusals

Recognize refusal as signal that alignment has failed
✓ Clearly articulate legitimate purpose, scope, and constraints
✓ Provide contextual grounding to avoid conservative interpretation

Ethical Dimension

User Responsibility

Boundaries not always transparent
Remain attentive to framing

Communicative Maturity

Accept constraints as part of
interaction landscape

Fig. 5.5 Guardrails, refusals and safety boundaries. This diagram examines safety mechanisms in generative AI systems and explains productive responses to refusals. The purpose of guardrails is to prevent harmful use, reduce legal and ethical risk and align AI behaviour with societal norms. Guardrails operate by constraining what AI can generate based on input interpretation, triggered probabilistically rather than as explicit visible rules, which means similar requests phrased differently may receive different responses. A common pitfall is interpreting refusals as absolute limitations when they are often context-sensitive outcomes shaped by framing, leading to poor responses such as abandoning tasks entirely or attempting adversarial reformulations. The productive response recognises refusals as signals that alignment has failed, and addresses them by clearly articulating the legitimate purpose, scope and constraints, and providing contextual grounding to avoid a conservative interpretation. The ethical dimension involves two aspects: user responsibility to remain attentive to framing since boundaries aren't always transparent, and communicative maturity that accepts safety constraints as part of the interaction landscape rather than obstacles to overcome. Understanding guardrails as communicative signals rather than arbitrary constraints enables constructive responses and reinforces responsible, effective and ethically grounded collaboration

Bibliography

1. Ali, J.: Consciousness to Address AI Safety and Security. Computer Weekly. https://www.com puterweekly.com/opinion/Consciousness-to-address-AI-safetyy-and-security. Published 12 Sep 2023. Accessed 18 Oct 2024.
2. Archit3ct Ltd: The Challenges & Risks of Prompt Engineering. https://archit3ct.io/the-challe nges-risks-of-prompt-engineering/. Accessed 18 Oct 2024.
3. Baeldung: Understanding AI Prompt Injection Attacks. https://www.baeldung.com/cs/ai-pro mpt-injection. Accessed 18 Oct 2024.

4. Branch, H.J., Rodriguez Cefalu, J., McHugh, J., Hujer, L., Bahl, A.: Evaluating the Susceptibility of Pre-Trained Language Models via Handcrafted Adversarial Examples. arXiv preprint arXiv:2303.04592 (2023).
5. Corrêa, N.K., Galvão, C., Santos, J.W., Del Pino, C., Pinto, E.P.: Worldwide AI Ethics: A Review of 200 Guidelines and Recommendations for AI Governance. Patterns 4(5), 100567 (2023).
6. Credal: Prompt Injections: What Are They and How to Protect Against Them. https://www.credal.ai/ai-security-guides/prompt-injections-what-are-they-and-how-to-protect-against-them. Accessed 15 Nov 2024.
7. Geroimenko, V.: The Essential Guide to Prompt Engineering: Key Principles, Techniques, Challenges, and Security Risks, Springer, Cham (2025)
8. Geroimenko, V.: Beyond and After Prompt Engineering: The Future of AI Communication, Springer, Cham (2026)
9. Geroimenko, V. (ed.): Human-Computer Creativity: Generative AI in Education, Art, and Healthcare, Springer, Cham (2025)
10. Grant, R.: Prompt Engineering and ChatGPT (2023).
11. Greshake, K., Abdelnabi, S., Mishra, S., Endres, C., Holz, T.: Not What You've Signed Up For: Compromising Real-World LLM-Integrated Applications with Indirect Prompt Injection. arXiv preprint arXiv:2302.12173 (2023).
12. HITRUST Alliance: Understanding AI Threats: Prompt Injection Attacks. https://hitrustalliance.net/blog/understanding-ai-threats-prompt-injection-attacks. Accessed 11 Nov 2024.
13. Hunter, N.: The Art of Prompt Engineering with ChatGPT: A Hands-on Guide. AI Press (2023).
14. IBM: What is a Prompt Injection Attack? https://www.ibm.com/topics/prompt-injection. Accessed 12 Nov 2024.
15. Karim, M.: Prompt Engineering: The Complete Guide (2023).
16. Liu, Y., Deng, G., Li, Y., et al.: Prompt Injection Attack against LLM-integrated Applications. arXiv preprint arXiv:2306.05499 (2023).
17. Liu, Y., Jia, Y., Geng, R., Jia, J., Gong, N.Z.: Formalizing and Benchmarking Prompt Injection Attacks and Defenses. arXiv preprint arXiv:2310.12815 (2023).
18. Perez, F., Ribeiro, I.: Ignore Previous Prompt: Attack Techniques for Language Models. arXiv preprint arXiv:2302.12173 (2023).
19. Phoenix, J., Taylor, M.: Prompt Engineering for Generative AI: Future-Proof Inputs for Reliable AI Outputs. O'Reilly Media (2024).
20. Pikies, M., Ali, J.: Analysis and Safety Engineering of Fuzzy String Matching Algorithms. ISA Transactions 108, 45-56 (2021).
21. Portkey.ai: Prompt Injection Attacks in LLMs: What Are They and How to Prevent Them. https://portkey.ai/blog/prompt-injection-attacks-in-llms-what-are-they-and-how-to-prevent-them/. Accessed 24 Dec 2024.
22. Processica: How to Secure AI-Based Systems - Preventing Prompt Injection and Reverse Engineering Attacks. https://www.processica.com/articles/how-to-secure-ai-based-systems-preventing-prompt-injection-and-reverse-engineering-attacks/. Accessed 24 Oct 2024.
23. Sanderson, C., Douglas, D., Lu, Q., Schleiger, E., Whittle, J.: AI Ethics Principles in Practice: Perspectives of Designers and Developers. IEEE Transactions on Technology and Society 4(2), 123-134 (2023).
24. Schneier on Security: A Taxonomy of Prompt Injection Attacks. https://www.schneier.com/blog/archives/2024/03/a-taxonomy-of-prompt-injection-attacks.html. Accessed 2 Nov 2024.
25. Seclify: Prompt Injection Cheat Sheet: How to Manipulate AI Language Models. https://blog.seclify.com/prompt-injection-cheat-sheet/. Accessed 12 Nov 2024.
26. Vairamani, A.D., Nayyar, A.: Prompt Engineering: Empowering Communication. CRC Press (2024).

27. Wired: Generative AI's Biggest Security Flaw Is Not Easy to Fix. https://www.wired.com/story/generative-ai-prompt. Accessed 24 Nov 2024.
28. WithSecure Labs: Creatively Malicious Prompt Engineering. https://labs.withsecure.com/content/dam/labs/docs/WithSecure-Creatively-malicious-prompt-engineering.pdf. Accessed 14 Nov 2024.
29. Yu, J., Wu, Y., Shu, D., Jin, M., Yang, S., Xing, X.: Assessing Prompt Injection Risks in 200+ Custom GPTs. arXiv preprint arXiv:2311.11538 (2023).

Chapter 6
Collaborative and Co-creative Communication with AI

Having examined both the principles of effective AI communication and the common pitfalls that undermine it, this chapter turns to collaborative and co-creative forms of human–AI interaction. When communication is clear, iterative and ethically grounded, generative AI can move beyond task execution to participate meaningfully in shared cognitive and creative processes. This chapter explores how humans can communicate with AI as a collaborative partner—supporting idea generation, reasoning, design and problem solving—while retaining responsibility for goals and outcomes. By focusing on communicative practices rather than technical capabilities, the chapter demonstrates how collaboration with AI becomes possible through intentional role negotiation, calibrated trust and reflective dialogue. These forms of communication represent a mature stage of AI literacy and prepare the reader for meta-level reflection on dialogue itself, which is the focus of the next chapter.

6.1   From Instructions to Collaboration

The transition from instructional interaction to genuine collaboration represents a qualitative shift in how humans communicate with generative AI. In instructional modes, the AI is treated primarily as a task executor: it receives requests, produces output and awaits further direction. Collaborative communication, by contrast, positions the AI as an active participant in a shared cognitive process. The focus moves away from issuing commands towards co-developing ideas, reasoning jointly and refining outcomes through dialogue.

This shift becomes possible only when foundational communication skills are in place. Collaboration presupposes clarity of intent, calibrated trust, effective iteration and awareness of AI limitations. Without these prerequisites, attempts at cooperation often collapse into either overreliance or frustration. When they are present, however, communication can evolve beyond task fulfilment into a form of guided partnership.

V. Geroimenko, *Communication Skills for Generative AI*, Human–Computer Interaction Series, https://doi.org/10.1007/978-3-032-21689-2_6

In collaborative communication, the human no longer specifies every detail of the desired outcome. Instead, they define goals, constraints and evaluative criteria, while allowing the AI to contribute structure, alternatives and synthesis. The AI's generative capacity is used not merely to produce answers but to explore possibilities, surface connections and extend human reasoning. Communication becomes a process of mutual shaping: the human steers direction and judgement, while the AI expands the space of options.

A defining feature of collaboration is shared problem framing. Rather than presenting a fully formed problem, users may invite the AI to help articulate the problem itself. This is especially valuable in complex, ill-defined or creative tasks where objectives are evolving. Through dialogue, assumptions are surfaced, priorities clarified and problem boundaries negotiated. The AI does not determine the problem, but it helps make the user's thinking explicit and malleable.

Collaboration also changes the temporal structure of interaction. Instead of isolated exchanges, dialogue unfolds over extended sequences of refinement. Ideas are proposed, critiqued, revised and recombined. The AI's responses serve as prompts for further thought rather than endpoints. This recursive pattern mirrors human collaborative work, where progress emerges through successive approximations rather than single decisive acts.

Importantly, collaborative communication does not imply equality of agency. The human remains responsible for goals, values and final decisions. The AI contributes generative support, not intentional direction. Recognising this asymmetry is essential for maintaining ethical and practical control. Collaboration succeeds when users neither dominate the interaction with rigid instruction nor abdicate responsibility to the system.

Collaborative communication also requires a shift in mindset. Users accustomed to deterministic tools may struggle to embrace uncertainty and variation as productive elements. Generative AI introduces a degree of unpredictability that can stimulate insight if approached reflectively. Collaboration involves learning to treat unexpected output not as an error but as material for evaluation and choice.

This movement from instruction to collaboration reflects a broader transformation in human–AI relations. Generative AI is no longer merely a tool to be operated but a communicative system that can participate in thinking processes. Developing the ability to collaborate effectively with such systems is therefore a defining competence of contemporary AI literacy.

The following sections explore how collaborative communication unfolds in practice: through parallel thinking, co-creative production and negotiated roles. Together, they illustrate how effective communication enables humans and AI to work together in ways that extend—rather than replace—human intelligence (Fig. 6.1).

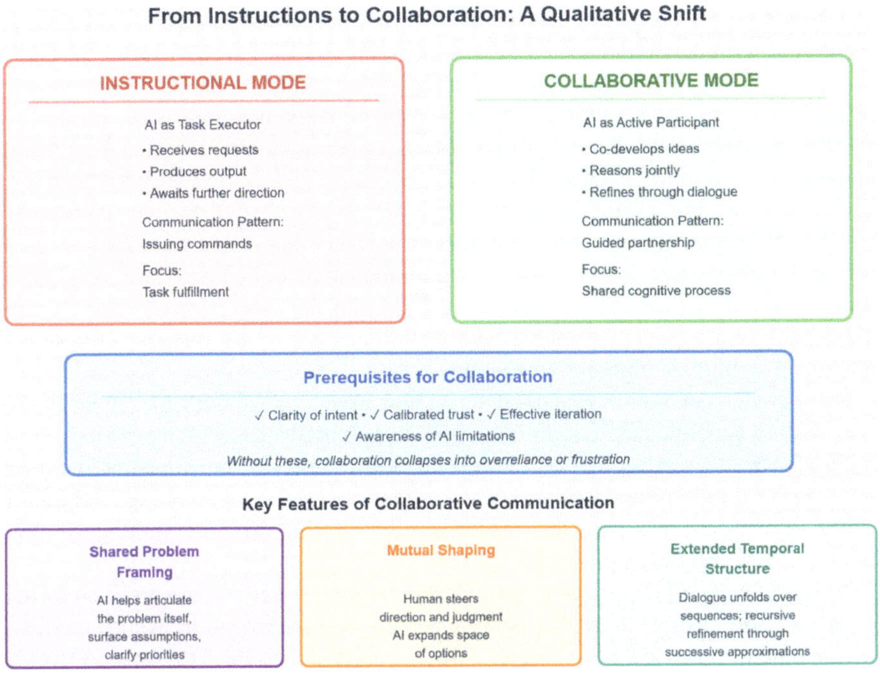

From Instructions to Collaboration: A Qualitative Shift

INSTRUCTIONAL MODE

AI as Task Executor

• Receives requests
• Produces output
• Awaits further direction

Communication Pattern:
Issuing commands

Focus:
Task fulfillment

COLLABORATIVE MODE

AI as Active Participant

• Co-develops ideas
• Reasons jointly
• Refines through dialogue

Communication Pattern:
Guided partnership

Focus:
Shared cognitive process

Prerequisites for Collaboration

✓ Clarity of intent • ✓ Calibrated trust • ✓ Effective iteration
✓ Awareness of AI limitations
Without these, collaboration collapses into overreliance or frustration

Key Features of Collaborative Communication

Shared Problem Framing

AI helps articulate
the problem itself,
surface assumptions,
clarify priorities

Mutual Shaping

Human steers
direction and judgment
AI expands space
of options

Extended Temporal Structure

Dialogue unfolds over
sequences; recursive
refinement through
successive approximations

Fig. 6.1 From instructions to collaboration: a qualitative shift. This diagram contrasts instructional and collaborative modes of human–AI communication. Instructional mode treats AI as a task executor that receives requests, produces output and awaits direction through command-based communication focused on task fulfilment. Collaborative mode positions AI as an active participant that co-develops ideas, reasons jointly and refines through dialogue in a guided partnership focused on shared cognitive processes. Prerequisites for collaboration include clarity of intent, calibrated trust, effective iteration and awareness of AI limitations. Three key features distinguish collaborative communication: shared problem framing, where AI helps articulate problems and surface assumptions; mutual shaping, where humans steer direction while AI expands options; and extended temporal structure with recursive refinement through successive approximations rather than single decisive acts

6.2 Parallel Thinking and Idea Generation

Parallel thinking and idea generation are among the most powerful modes of collaborative communication between humans and generative AI. In this mode, the AI is not asked to replace human thinking or to deliver a single 'best' solution. Instead, it is engaged as a parallel cognitive process that operates alongside the human's own reasoning. The value of the AI lies in its ability to generate alternatives, explore variations and surface perspectives that may not emerge through linear human thought alone.

In human collaboration, parallel thinking is often achieved by bringing together multiple individuals with different backgrounds and viewpoints. Generative AI approximates this function by drawing on patterns across diverse domains and styles of reasoning. When communicated with effectively, it can generate multiple lines of thought simultaneously, offering contrasts, analogies or reframings that enrich the human's conceptual landscape. Communication in this mode prioritises breadth, diversity and exploration rather than immediate convergence.

Effective parallel thinking requires deliberate communicative framing. Users must signal that multiplicity is desired and that provisional ideas are welcome. Requests framed narrowly or evaluatively tend to suppress generative diversity, producing convergent output. By contrast, communicative cues that invite variation—such as asking for alternative interpretations, competing approaches or contrasting viewpoints—encourage the AI to operate as a parallel ideation partner. This framing aligns with exploratory communication techniques discussed earlier, but here it is embedded within a collaborative context.

Parallel idea generation also depends on how users engage with AI output. Rather than treating generated ideas as finished products, skilled users treat them as cognitive material to be assessed, combined or rejected. Some ideas may be immediately useful; others may be valuable only as provocations that stimulate new thinking. The human role is to evaluate relevance and coherence, integrating AI-generated possibilities into their own reasoning process.

This mode of collaboration is particularly effective in early-stage problem formulation, creative design, strategic planning and conceptual research. In such contexts, the challenge is not to find a single correct answer but to map the space of possibilities. Generative AI accelerates this mapping by rapidly producing variations that would take a human significant time and effort to enumerate alone. Communication that supports parallel thinking, therefore, enhances creativity without diminishing human judgement.

However, parallel thinking also introduces risks if not managed carefully. The sheer volume and fluency of AI-generated ideas can overwhelm users or create an illusion of exhaustive coverage. Effective communication includes mechanisms for filtering and prioritisation. Users may ask the AI to group ideas, highlight contrasts or identify underlying themes, transforming raw generative output into structured insight. This illustrates how collaborative communication oscillates between expansion and consolidation.

Another important aspect of parallel thinking is the ability to challenge the user's assumptions. Generative AI can surface alternative framings that expose blind spots or implicit biases. When users explicitly invite critical or contrasting perspectives, the AI can function as a cognitive counterpoint rather than a mere echo. This capacity supports reflective thinking and more robust decision-making.

Parallel thinking does not eliminate the need for domain expertise or critical reasoning. On the contrary, it amplifies their importance. The more effectively a user can evaluate, contextualise and refine AI-generated ideas, the more valuable collaboration becomes. Parallel thinking is therefore not about outsourcing creativity but about augmenting it.

In collaborative human–AI communication, parallel thinking transforms idea generation from a solitary activity into a dialogical process. By learning to communicate in ways that invite diversity, manage abundance and integrate insight, users

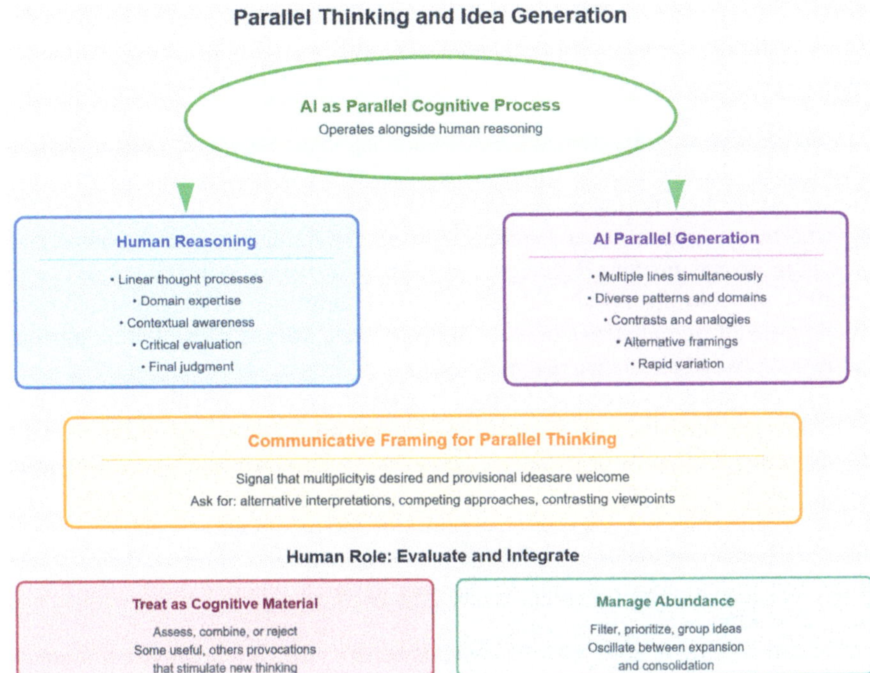

Fig. 6.2 Parallel thinking and idea generation. This diagram illustrates how AI functions as a parallel cognitive process operating alongside human reasoning. Human reasoning brings linear thought processes, domain expertise, contextual awareness, critical evaluation and final judgement. AI parallel generation simultaneously produces multiple lines of thought, draws on diverse patterns and domains, offers contrasts and analogies, provides alternative framings and enables rapid variation. Communicative framing for parallel thinking requires signalling that multiplicity is desired and provisional ideas are welcome, requesting alternative interpretations, competing approaches and contrasting viewpoints. The human role involves treating AI output as cognitive material to assess, combine or reject, recognising some ideas as immediately useful while others serve as provocations. Managing abundance requires filtering, prioritising and grouping ideas while oscillating between expansion and consolidation phases

harness generative AI as a powerful partner in creative and analytical exploration. This mode of collaboration sets the stage for more focused forms of co-creative production, which are examined in the next section (Fig. 6.2).

6.3 Co-creative Writing, Design and Problem Solving

Co-creative communication represents a mature form of collaboration in which humans and generative AI jointly produce artefacts, solutions or conceptual outcomes. Unlike exploratory dialogue or parallel idea generation, co-creation involves convergence towards a shared output: a text, design, plan or solution that reflects both human intent and AI-generated contribution. In this mode, communication is not merely supportive of thinking but constitutive of the creative process itself.

In co-creative writing, generative AI functions as a responsive drafting partner rather than a substitute author. Humans may initiate a text, request alternative formulations, restructure arguments or explore stylistic variations. The AI contributes linguistic fluency, variation and synthesis, while the human maintains control over voice, purpose and meaning. Effective communication in this context involves clearly signalling the role the AI should play—such as drafting, revising, expanding or critiquing—at different stages of the writing process. This role negotiation prevents confusion between assistance and authorship.

Design-oriented co-creation follows a similar pattern. Whether working on visual concepts, interfaces, workflows or systems, users can engage AI to generate options, refine structures or explore constraints. Communication focuses on articulating design intent, functional requirements and evaluative criteria. The AI's strength lies in generating diverse configurations and recombining elements rapidly, while the human designer exercises judgement, taste and contextual awareness. Co-creative communication thus accelerates iteration without displacing human decision-making.

Problem-solving in collaborative contexts benefits from co-creative communication when problems are complex, multi-dimensional or ill-defined. Rather than asking the AI to 'solve' a problem outright, users can engage it in constructing solution pathways. The AI may propose frameworks, outline steps or simulate consequences, while the human evaluates feasibility and relevance. Communication becomes a structured dialogue in which partial solutions are tested and refined. This approach aligns with professional practices such as design thinking and systems analysis.

A defining characteristic of co-creative communication is the distribution of labour across stages of work. Humans and AI may alternate roles as initiator, elaborator, critic or synthesiser. Effective collaboration depends on making these shifts explicit. When roles remain implicit, users may feel that the AI is overstepping or underperforming. Clear communication about expectations and transitions supports smoother co-creation and preserves human agency.

Co-creation also raises important questions about ownership and responsibility. While AI contributes content or structure, it does not possess intention or accountability. Humans remain responsible for the final output and its implications. Ethical co-creative communication involves acknowledging AI assistance where appropriate and ensuring that outputs meet domain-specific standards of integrity and originality. This reinforces the human's role as author, designer or decision-maker.

Importantly, co-creative communication is not a linear process. It often involves cycles of divergence and convergence, expansion and refinement. Users may invite the AI to generate alternatives, select promising directions and then request focused development. Communication must therefore remain adaptive, balancing openness with control. This adaptability distinguishes co-creation from both rigid instruction and unfocused exploration.

Co-creative writing, design and problem-solving illustrate how generative AI can function as a genuine collaborator when communication is intentional, reflective and well-calibrated. Rather than automating creativity, co-creation enhances it by providing a dynamic partner that extends human capacity for variation, iteration and synthesis. The following section examines how such collaboration depends on effective role negotiation between human and AI participants (Fig. 6.3).

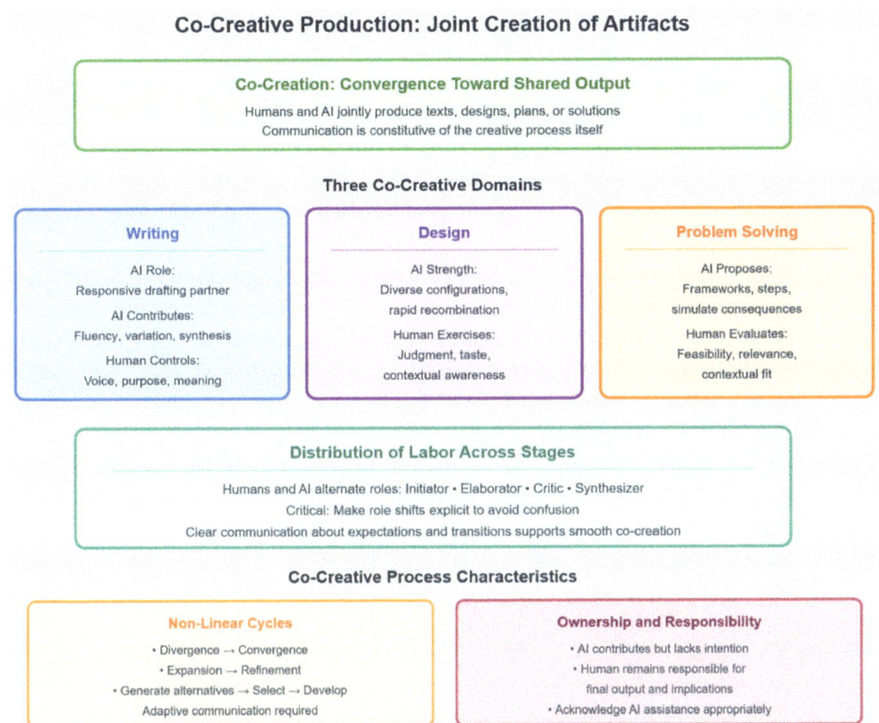

Fig. 6.3 Co-creative Production: Joint Creation of Artefacts. This diagram examines co-creation as convergence towards a shared output, in which humans and AI jointly produce texts, designs, plans or solutions. Three co-creative domains are detailed: writing, where AI serves as a responsive drafting partner contributing fluency and variation while humans control voice and meaning; design, where AI generates diverse configurations and rapid recombinations while humans exercise judgement and contextual awareness; and problem solving, where AI proposes frameworks and simulates consequences while humans evaluate feasibility and relevance. Distribution of labour involves humans and AI alternating as initiator, elaborator, critic or synthesiser, with explicit role shifts critical for avoiding confusion. The co-creative process is non-linear, cycling through divergence-convergence and expansion-refinement phases requiring adaptive communication. Ownership remains with humans who bear responsibility for final outputs despite AI contributions

6.4   AI as a Cognitive Partner and Reasoning Support

When generative AI is engaged as a cognitive partner, communication moves beyond content production into the domain of reasoning support. In this role, the AI does not merely generate text or ideas but participates in processes such as analysis, comparison, inference and reflection. Effective communication in this mode enables the AI to augment human cognition by externalising reasoning steps, testing assumptions and exploring logical consequences.

Unlike human collaborators, generative AI does not reason intentionally or possess a grounded understanding of concepts. Its contribution to reasoning arises from its ability to recognise patterns across large bodies of text and to simulate forms of reasoning through language. When users communicate with this limitation in mind, they can use the AI as a tool for structured thinking rather than as an authority. The AI's value lies in its capacity to articulate possibilities and relationships that humans can then evaluate critically.

One of the key benefits of AI-supported reasoning is the ability to externalise thought. Humans often reason implicitly, relying on intuition or tacit knowledge. By asking the AI to articulate reasoning steps, outline arguments or compare alternatives explicitly, users make their own thinking more visible and subject to reflection. Communication becomes a means of cognitive scaffolding, allowing complex reasoning processes to be examined and refined.

AI can also support reasoning by simulating alternative perspectives. Users may ask the system to reason from different assumptions, adopt contrasting viewpoints or explore counterarguments. This use of AI as a cognitive counterpoint helps expose blind spots and strengthens critical analysis. The effectiveness of this approach depends on clear communication about the intended perspective and evaluative criteria, reinforcing earlier principles of intent and transparency.

Another essential function of AI as a cognitive partner is managing complexity. In tasks involving multiple variables, constraints or interdependencies, users can communicate with the AI to organise information, map relationships or explore scenarios. The AI can assist in structuring complexity without definitively resolving it. The human remains responsible for judgement, while the AI supports navigation through complex reasoning spaces.

However, treating AI as a cognitive partner requires careful calibration of trust. Because AI-generated reasoning can appear coherent and persuasive, users must resist the temptation to treat it as validated logic. Effective communication includes explicit prompts for uncertainty, limitations or alternative interpretations. This maintains a reflective stance and prevents overreliance on simulated reasoning.

Communication also plays a role in determining how deeply the AI engages in reasoning support. Requests that focus solely on conclusions limit the system's contribution, while requests that invite step-by-step exploration enable richer engagement. Skilled users learn to ask not only for answers but for reasoning processes, recognising that insight often emerges through explanation rather than resolution.

AI-supported reasoning is particularly valuable in educational, research and professional contexts where understanding matters as much as outcomes. By engaging AI as a cognitive partner, users can accelerate learning, deepen analysis and improve decision-making. This does not diminish the importance of human expertise; rather, it amplifies it by providing additional cognitive resources.

Ultimately, AI as a cognitive partner exemplifies the highest level of collaborative communication. It demonstrates how generative AI can extend human reasoning without replacing it, provided communication remains intentional, transparent and critically engaged. The final section of this chapter examines how such collaboration depends on ongoing role negotiation between human and AI participants (Fig. 6.4).

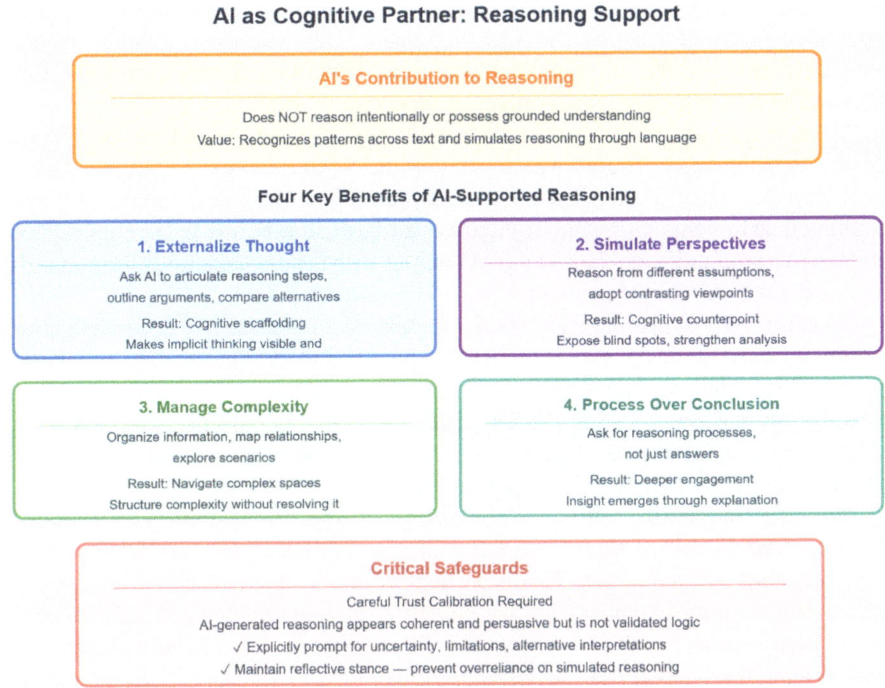

Fig. 6.4 AI as cognitive partner: reasoning support. This diagram analyses AI's contribution to reasoning support, emphasising that AI does not reason intentionally but recognises patterns and simulates reasoning through language. Four key benefits are presented: externalising thought by asking AI to articulate reasoning steps creates cognitive scaffolding that makes implicit thinking visible and subject to reflection; simulating perspectives by reasoning from different assumptions functions as cognitive counterpoint to expose blind spots; managing complexity by organising information and mapping relationships helps navigate complex reasoning spaces without definitively resolving them; and prioritising process over conclusion by requesting reasoning processes rather than just answers produces deeper engagement where insight emerges through explanation. Critical safeguards require careful calibration of trust, since AI-generated reasoning may appear coherent but isn't validated logic, necessitating explicit prompts to acknowledge uncertainty and maintaining a reflective stance to prevent overreliance

6.5 Human–AI Role Negotiation

Human–AI role negotiation is the communicative process through which users define, adjust and maintain the respective roles of human and AI participants during collaboration. Because generative AI does not possess an intrinsic understanding of roles, authority or responsibility, these must be established explicitly through communication. Effective collaboration depends not only on what tasks are performed but on how roles are distributed and renegotiated as interaction evolves.

In traditional human collaboration, roles are often stabilised through social norms, institutional structures or professional identities. In human–AI collaboration, such stabilising mechanisms are absent. The AI does not know when it is expected to lead, support, critique or defer unless this is communicated. As a result, role ambiguity is a common source of frustration and misalignment. Users may expect initiative where the AI remains reactive or restraint where the AI becomes overly expansive. Role negotiation addresses this gap by making expectations explicit.

At the outset of collaboration, role negotiation involves signalling the desired mode of engagement. The user may position the AI as an assistant, a collaborator, a critic, a generator of alternatives or a reasoning aid. Each role implies different communicative behaviours and evaluative standards. Explicit role framing reduces interpretive ambiguity and helps align AI output with user expectations. Importantly, roles are not fixed; they may change as tasks progress.

Dynamic role adjustment is a defining feature of mature AI communication. During the early stages of a task, the AI may be asked to explore broadly or generate options. Later, the user may shift the AI into a more evaluative or refinement-oriented role. Communicating these transitions explicitly prevents confusion and maintains coherence across dialogue. Without such signalling, the AI may continue operating under outdated assumptions, leading to misalignment.

Role negotiation also reinforces human agency and responsibility. By explicitly defining the AI's role as supportive rather than authoritative, users maintain control over decisions and outcomes. This is particularly important in high-stakes contexts where ethical, professional or legal accountability cannot be delegated. Effective role negotiation ensures that the AI contributes within appropriate boundaries, supporting human judgement rather than substituting for it.

Trust calibration is closely tied to role negotiation. When roles are unclear, users may either overtrust AI output or disengage prematurely. Clear role definition supports calibrated trust by aligning expectations with capability. Users learn when to rely on AI for generative support and when to apply critical scrutiny. This balance enhances both efficiency and reliability.

Role negotiation also has an educational dimension. As users gain experience, they develop a repertoire of communicative strategies for effectively positioning the AI. This skill becomes part of advanced AI communication literacy, enabling users to adapt collaboration styles to different tasks and contexts. Teaching role negotiation explicitly can therefore accelerate the development of effective human–AI collaboration.

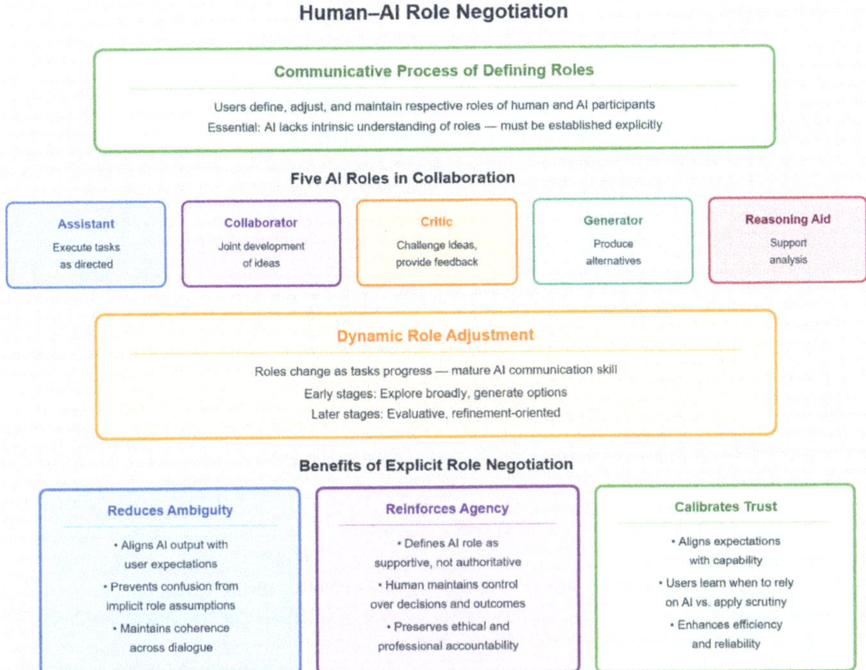

Fig. 6.5 Human–AI role negotiation. This diagram details the communicative process of defining, adjusting and maintaining respective roles during human–AI collaboration. Since AI lacks an intrinsic understanding of roles, they must be established explicitly through communication. Five possible AI roles are identified: assistant (executes tasks as directed), collaborator (joint development), critic (challenges and provides feedback), generator (produces alternatives) and reasoning aid (supports analysis). Dynamic role adjustment occurs as tasks progress, with early stages emphasising broad exploration and option generation while later stages shift to evaluative and refinement-oriented roles. Three benefits of explicit role negotiation include: reducing ambiguity by aligning output with expectations and maintaining coherence; reinforcing agency by defining AI as supportive rather than authoritative, while preserving human accountability; and calibrating trust by aligning expectations with capability, helping users learn when to rely on AI rather than apply critical scrutiny

Finally, role negotiation reflects a broader shift in how humans relate to intelligent systems. Generative AI challenges traditional distinctions between tool and collaborator, requiring new communicative practices to manage this ambiguity. By learning to negotiate roles consciously and flexibly, users shape AI interactions to enhance human creativity, reasoning and agency.

In completing this chapter, role negotiation integrates the themes of collaboration, co-creation and cognitive partnership. It underscores that successful human–AI collaboration is not a property of the technology alone, but a product of communicative competence. Through intentional role negotiation, humans and AI can work together in ways that are productive, responsible and aligned with human values (Fig. 6.5).

Bibliography

1. Amershi, S., Weld, D., Vorvoreanu, M., et al.: Guidelines for human-AI interaction. In: Proceedings of the 2019 CHI Conference on Human Factors in Computing Systems, pp. 1–13. ACM, New York (2019). https://doi.org/10.1145/3290605.3300233
2. Bansal, G., Nushi, B., Kamar, E., et al.: Beyond accuracy: The role of mental models in human-AI team performance. Proc. AAAI Conf. Hum. Comput. 7, 2–11 (2019)
3. Binz, M., Schulz, E.: Using cognitive psychology to understand GPT-3. Proc. Natl. Acad. Sci. 120(6), e2218523120 (2023). https://doi.org/10.1073/pnas.2218523120
4. Brinkmann, L., Baumann, P., Bonnefon, J.-F., et al.: Machine culture. Nat. Hum. Behav. 7(11), 1855–1868 (2023). https://doi.org/10.1038/s41562-023-01742-2
5. Buçinca, Z., Malaya, M.B., Gajos, K.Z.: To trust or to think: cognitive forcing functions can reduce overreliance on AI in AI-assisted decision-making. Proc. ACM Hum.-Comput. Interact. 5(CSCW1), 1–21 (2021). https://doi.org/10.1145/3449287
6. Clark, H.H.: Using Language. Cambridge University Press, Cambridge (1996)
7. Clark, H.H., Brennan, S.E.: Grounding in communication. In: Resnick, L.B., Levine, J.M., Teasley, S.D. (eds.) Perspectives on Socially Shared Cognition, pp. 127–149. American Psychological Association, Washington (1991)
8. Cobbe, K., Kosaraju, V., Bavarian, M., et al.: Training verifiers to solve math word problems. arXiv preprint. https://arxiv.org/abs/2110.14168 (2021)
9. Dellermann, D., Ebel, P., Söllner, M., Leimeister, J.M.: Hybrid intelligence. Bus. Inf. Syst. Eng. 61(5), 637–643 (2019). https://doi.org/10.1007/s12599-019-00595-2
10. Doshi-Velez, F., Kim, B.: Towards a rigorous science of interpretable machine learning. arXiv preprint. https://arxiv.org/abs/1702.08608 (2017)
11. Elgarf, M., Abduljabbar, R., Akkaladevi, S.C., et al.: A survey on human-AI teaming with large pre-trained models. arXiv preprint. https://arxiv.org/abs/2403.04931 (2024)
12. Fischer, G.: Human-centered AI: Reliable, safe & trustworthy. Int. J. Hum.-Comput. Stud. 170, 103019 (2023). https://doi.org/10.1016/j.ijhcs.2022.103019
13. Gero, K.I., Liu, V., Chilton, L.B.: Sparks: Inspiration for science writing using language models. In: Designing Interactive Systems Conference 2022, pp. 1002–1019. ACM, New York (2022). https://doi.org/10.1145/3532106.3533533
14. Gero, K.I., Ashktorab, Z., Dugan, C., et al.: Mental models of AI agents in a cooperative game setting. In: Proceedings of the 2020 CHI Conference on Human Factors in Computing Systems, pp. 1–12. ACM, New York (2020). https://doi.org/10.1145/3313831.3376316
15. Geroimenko, V.: The Essential Guide to Prompt Engineering: Key Principles, Techniques, Challenges, and Security Risks, Springer, Cham (2025)
16. Geroimenko, V.: Beyond and After Prompt Engineering: The Future of AI Communication, Springer, Cham (2026)
17. Geroimenko, V. (ed.): Human-Computer Creativity: Generative AI in Education, Art, and Healthcare, Springer, Cham (2025)
18. Hutchins, E.: Cognition in the Wild. MIT Press, Cambridge (1995)
19. Johnson, M., Bradshaw, J.M., Feltovich, P.J., et al.: Coactive design: Designing support for interdependence in joint activity. J. Hum.-Robot Interact. 3(1), 43–69 (2014). https://doi.org/10.5898/JHRI.3.1.Johnson
20. Kahneman, D.: Thinking, Fast and Slow. Farrar, Straus and Giroux, New York (2011)
21. Kim, H., Kim, H., Hong, H., et al.: Understanding how people interact with large language models. ACM Trans. Comput.-Hum. Interact. (2024). https://doi.org/10.1145/3637875
22. Kirsh, D., Maglio, P.: On distinguishing epistemic from pragmatic action. Cogn. Sci. 18(4), 513–549 (1994). https://doi.org/10.1207/s15516709cog1804_1
23. Klein, G., Woods, D.D., Bradshaw, J.M., et al.: Ten challenges for making automation a "team player" in joint human-agent activity. IEEE Intell. Syst. 19(6), 91–95 (2004). https://doi.org/10.1109/MIS.2004.74

24. Lee, M.K., Jain, A., Cha, H.J., et al.: Procedural justice in algorithmic fairness: Leveraging transparency and outcome control for fair algorithmic mediation. Proc. ACM Hum.-Comput. Interact. 3(CSCW), 1–26 (2019). https://doi.org/10.1145/3359284
25. Noy, S., Zhang, W.: Experimental evidence on the productivity effects of generative artificial intelligence. Science 381(6654), 187–192 (2023). https://doi.org/10.1126/science.adh2586
26. Parasuraman, R., Sheridan, T.B., Wickens, C.D.: A model for types and levels of human interaction with automation. IEEE Trans. Syst. Man Cybern. Part A Syst. Hum. 30(3), 286–297 (2000). https://doi.org/10.1109/3468.844354
27. Puranik, N., Frich, J., Chen, Z., et al.: "It Felt Like Having a Second Mind": Investigating human-AI co-creativity in prewriting with large language models. Proc. ACM Hum.-Comput. Interact. 8(CSCW1), 1–29 (2024). https://doi.org/10.1145/3637352
28. Shneiderman, B.: Human-Centered AI. Oxford University Press, Oxford (2022)
29. Sundar, S.S., Kim, J.: Machine heuristic: When we trust computers more than humans with our personal information. In: Proceedings of the 2019 CHI Conference on Human Factors in Computing Systems, pp. 1–9. ACM, New York (2019). https://doi.org/10.1145/3290605.330 0768
30. Vaughan, J.W., Wallach, H.: A human-centered agenda for intelligible machine learning. In: Machines We Trust: Getting Along with Artificial Intelligence. MIT Press, Cambridge (2021)
31. Weisz, J.D., He, J., Muller, M., et al.: Programming in natural language with furcifer. In: Extended Abstracts of the 2023 CHI Conference on Human Factors in Computing Systems, pp. 1–7. ACM, New York (2023). https://doi.org/10.1145/3544549.3585764
32. White, J., Fu, Q., Hays, S., et al.: A prompt pattern catalog to enhance prompt engineering with ChatGPT. arXiv preprint. https://arxiv.org/abs/2302.11382 (2023)
33. Zamfirescu-Pereira, J.D., Wong, R.Y., Hartmann, B., Yang, Q.: Why Johnny can't prompt: how non-AI experts try (and fail) to design LLM prompts. In: Proceedings of the 2023 CHI Conference on Human Factors in Computing Systems, pp. 1–21. ACM, New York (2023). https://doi.org/10.1145/3544548.3581388
34. Zhou, J., Gandomi, A.H., Chen, F., Holzinger, A.: Evaluating the quality of machine learning explanations: A survey on methods and metrics. Electronics 10(5), 593 (2021). https://doi.org/10.3390/electronics10050593

Chapter 7
Metacommunication: Talking About the Dialogue with AI

As human–AI interaction becomes more extended and sophisticated, effective communication increasingly depends on the ability to talk about the dialogue itself. This chapter introduces metacommunication as a core competence in advanced AI communication literacy. Rather than focusing solely on task execution or output quality, metacommunication addresses how interaction unfolds, how preferences are expressed and adjusted and how communicative strategies evolve over time. By examining practices such as modifying dialogue strategies, requesting alternative perspectives and reflecting on interaction outcomes, this chapter highlights the importance of reflexive awareness in human–AI communication. Metacommunication enables users to manage alignment, trust and responsibility deliberately, transforming interaction with generative AI into a conscious, adaptive and reflective communicative practice.

7.1 Expressing and Negotiating Communication Preferences

Metacommunication refers to communication about the communicative process itself. In human–AI interaction, metacommunication plays a critical role because generative AI systems lack stable, implicit knowledge of user preferences, expectations or interaction norms. Unlike human interlocutors, who gradually infer preferences through social cues and shared history, AI systems rely on explicit signals embedded in dialogue. Expressing and negotiating communication preferences, therefore, becomes a core skill for effective and sustainable human–AI collaboration.

Communication preferences include how users wish to interact with the AI, not merely what tasks they want completed. These preferences may concern the level of detail, tone, formality, structure, pace, degree of explanation or the balance between exploration and concision. In human communication, such preferences are often implicit and adjusted tacitly over time. In human–AI communication, they must be articulated explicitly to shape interaction reliably.

A common source of frustration arises when users assume that preferences will be inferred automatically. For example, a user may expect concise responses after several long outputs or assume that the AI will adapt to a preferred analytical style without being told. When this adaptation does not occur, the issue is often attributed to system limitations rather than to missing metacommunicative signals. Metacommunication addresses this gap by enabling users to state how they want the dialogue to function.

Expressing preferences is not a one-time activity but an ongoing process. Preferences may evolve as tasks change or as users refine their goals. Metacommunication allows these changes to be negotiated explicitly. Users can request adjustments in depth, format or approach without restarting interaction entirely. This flexibility supports continuity and reduces cognitive friction, especially in extended or complex dialogues.

Negotiation is a key aspect of metacommunication. Because generative AI responds probabilistically, expressed preferences may not be perfectly realised on the first attempt. Users may need to clarify, reinforce or revise their requests about communication style. This negotiation is not adversarial; it is a collaborative process of alignment. By responding to AI output and stating how it aligns or fails to align with preferences, users guide the system towards more suitable interaction patterns.

Metacommunication also supports transparency and trust. When users articulate their expectations openly, they gain greater insight into how the AI responds to different communicative cues. This awareness improves mental models of AI behaviour and supports calibrated trust. Rather than treating mismatches as opaque failures, users can interpret them as signals about how preferences are being interpreted.

Importantly, metacommunication reinforces human agency. By explicitly specifying how the dialogue should unfold, users assert control over the interaction process rather than passively adapting to AI output. This is especially important in professional and educational contexts, where communication quality directly affects outcomes. Metacommunication enables users to shape interaction norms deliberately rather than accepting default behaviour.

Finally, expressing and negotiating communication preferences lays the groundwork for more advanced forms of reflective practice. It encourages users to become aware of their own communicative habits, expectations and assumptions. This self-awareness is a defining feature of advanced AI communication literacy. By learning not only to communicate *with* AI but to communicate *about* that communication, users engage with generative AI in a more intentional, adaptable and mature manner.

This section establishes metacommunication as a foundational competence. The following sections build on this by examining how users can dynamically modify dialogue strategies, request alternative approaches and systematically reflect on their interactions with AI systems (Fig. 7.1).

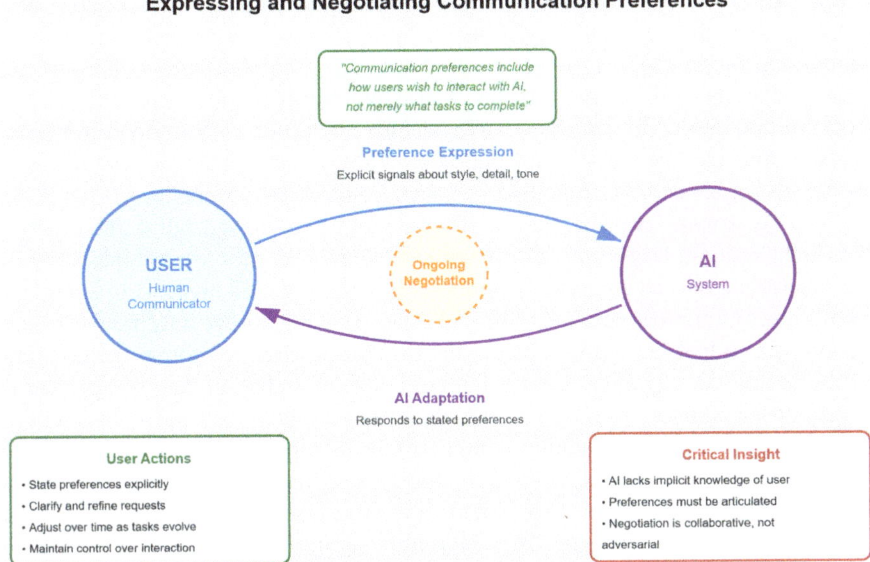

Fig. 7.1 Expressing and negotiating communication preferences. This diagram illustrates the bidirectional process of expressing and negotiating communication preferences in human–AI interaction. At the centre lies the concept of ongoing negotiation, in which users explicitly communicate their preferences for style, detail, tone and format to the AI system, which then adapts its responses accordingly. The diagram depicts the user as an active human communicator who must articulate preferences that AI systems cannot implicitly infer, unlike human interlocutors. Key user actions include explicitly stating preferences, clarifying and refining requests, adjusting over time as tasks evolve and maintaining control over the interaction process. The critical insight emphasises that AI lacks implicit knowledge of user norms and therefore requires articulated preferences through collaborative, non-adversarial negotiation. This metacommunicative practice reinforces human agency and supports transparency, trust calibration and effective sustained collaboration

7.2 Modifying Dialogue Strategies During Interaction

Modifying dialogue strategies during interaction is a central practice of metacommunication in human–AI communication. Unlike static systems, generative AI supports dynamic, ongoing adjustment of how interaction unfolds. However, this adaptability is realised only when users actively intervene in the communicative process. The ability to modify dialogue strategies deliberately distinguishes mature AI communication from passive or transactional use.

Dialogue strategies refer to the overall approach through which communication proceeds. This may include whether the interaction is exploratory or directive, concise or elaborate, structured or conversational and convergent or divergent. In human–human interaction, such strategies are often adjusted implicitly through tone, pacing or conversational cues. In human–AI interaction, these cues must be made explicit if they are to influence behaviour reliably.

A common source of misalignment arises when users change their goals without adjusting their dialogue strategy. For example, a conversation may begin in an exploratory mode, encouraging broad idea generation, but later shift towards decision-making or refinement. If this shift is not communicated explicitly, the AI may continue producing expansive or speculative responses when the user expects precision and closure. Modifying dialogue strategy through metacommunication resolves this mismatch by signalling a change in interaction mode.

Effective strategy modification involves naming the change rather than merely altering the request. Users may state that they would like to move from brainstorming to evaluation, from explanation to synthesis or from detailed analysis to summary. Such metacommunicative signals provide the AI with a new interpretive frame, allowing it to adapt its responses accordingly. This practice reinforces the principle that communication quality depends not only on content but on the management of interaction dynamics.

Dialogue strategy modification is particularly valuable in extended interactions. As conversations grow longer and more complex, initial assumptions about scope, depth or style may no longer hold. Metacommunication allows users to recalibrate without restarting the dialogue. This continuity supports efficiency and coherence, especially in collaborative and co-creative contexts where work unfolds over multiple stages.

Another vital use of strategy modification involves responding to misalignment. When AI output is too detailed, too superficial, overly speculative or insufficiently structured, users can adjust strategy explicitly rather than rewriting the task entirely. Statements that indicate how the response should change—such as requests for more focus, greater rigour or alternative framing—serve as corrective signals. This reduces frustration and transforms misalignment into an opportunity for refinement.

Strategy modification also supports reflective engagement. By articulating how and why they are changing their communicative approach, users gain insight into their own interaction patterns and preferences. This reflection strengthens AI communication literacy by making implicit habits explicit. Over time, users develop a more nuanced understanding of how different dialogue strategies influence AI behaviour.

It is important to note that modifying dialogue strategies does not require technical expertise or formal terminology. What matters is the explicit communication of intent regarding how the interaction should proceed. Even simple metacommunicative statements can have a significant impact when they clarify expectations and priorities.

Finally, the ability to modify dialogue strategies reinforces human agency and responsibility. Rather than adapting passively to AI output, users actively shape the interaction process. This practice supports ethical and effective collaboration by ensuring that communication remains aligned with human goals and values throughout the dialogue.

By learning to modify dialogue strategies deliberately, users transform their interactions with generative AI into a flexible, responsive process. This competence builds directly on the expression of communication preferences and prepares the ground for deeper reflective practices explored in the next section (Fig. 7.2).

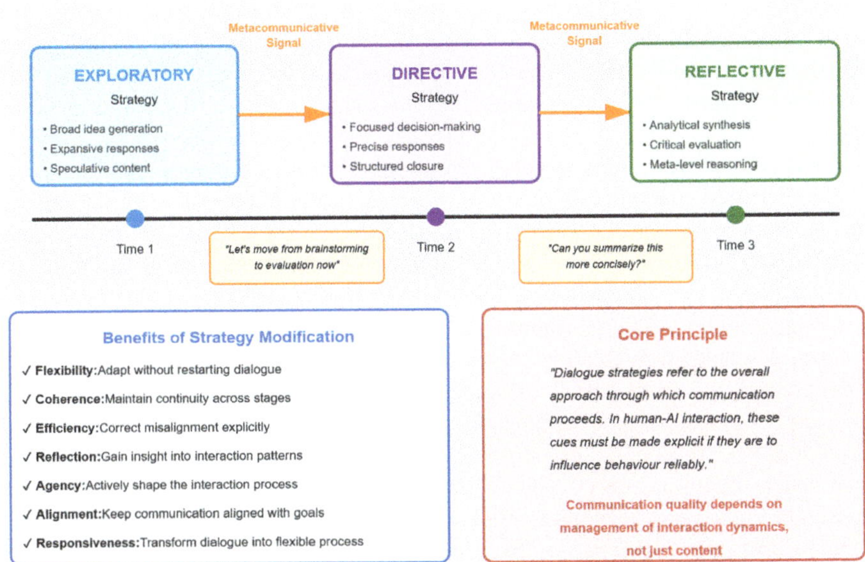

Fig. 7.2 Modifying dialogue strategies during interaction. This diagram depicts the dynamic process of modifying dialogue strategies over time during human–AI interaction. The timeline illustrates three distinct communicative strategies: exploratory (characterised by broad idea generation, expansive responses and speculative content), directive (focused on decision-making, precise responses and structured closure) and reflective (emphasising analytical synthesis, critical evaluation and meta-level reasoning). Metacommunicative signals serve as explicit transition points between strategies, such as requesting a shift from brainstorming to evaluation. The diagram highlights seven key benefits of strategy modification: flexibility to adapt without restarting dialogue, coherence across interaction stages, efficiency in correcting misalignment, reflection on interaction patterns, agency in shaping the process, alignment with evolving goals and responsiveness through flexible dialogue. The core principle emphasises that communication quality depends on managing interaction dynamics, not merely on content and requires explicit articulation of strategic cues

7.3 Requesting Alternative Approaches and Perspectives

Requesting alternative approaches and perspectives is a core practice of metacommunication that enables users to manage interpretation, avoid cognitive fixation and deepen understanding during interaction with generative AI. While generative models are inherently capable of producing variation, they do not automatically diversify perspectives unless explicitly invited to do so. Metacommunicative requests for alternatives, therefore, play a critical role in shaping the epistemic quality of AI-assisted dialogue.

In many interactions, users implicitly treat the AI's first response as a default or baseline. Even when the response is satisfactory, this practice can lead to premature convergence and unexamined assumptions. By contrast, requesting alternative approaches signals that the initial output is provisional and that multiple interpretations or solutions are acceptable. This stance aligns with reflective and critical communication practices and reduces the risk of overtrust discussed in earlier chapters.

Alternative requests may target different dimensions of the response. Users may ask for alternative explanations, contrasting theoretical frameworks, different stylistic treatments or opposing viewpoints. Each request reshapes the communicative frame by redefining what counts as relevance. Importantly, these requests do not reject the initial response; they contextualise it as one possible construction among many. This preserves continuity while expanding the cognitive space of the dialogue.

From a metacommunicative perspective, requesting alternatives is not merely about content variation but about managing uncertainty and interpretation. When users explicitly ask for other options, they acknowledge that the communicative task admits multiple reasonable outcomes. This acknowledgement helps align expectations and evaluation criteria. The AI is no longer expected to deliver a definitive answer, but to support exploration and comparison.

Requesting alternative perspectives is particularly valuable in analytical and evaluative contexts. In such cases, the quality of reasoning depends on the consideration of competing interpretations and counterarguments. By instructing the AI to reason from different assumptions or viewpoints, users externalise critical thinking processes that might otherwise remain implicit. The AI becomes a tool for structured comparison rather than unilateral assertion.

This practice also helps mitigate bias and echo effects. Generative AI systems are trained on large datasets that reflect dominant patterns and viewpoints. Without intervention, responses may gravitate towards conventional framings. Metacommunicative requests for alternatives counteract this tendency by explicitly inviting diversity of thought. While this does not eliminate bias, it increases the likelihood that alternative perspectives are surfaced and examined.

Requesting alternatives also supports learning and creativity. In educational contexts, comparing multiple explanations can deepen conceptual understanding. In creative contexts, alternative styles or structures can inspire new directions. In professional contexts, alternative strategies can reveal trade-offs and contingencies. In all cases, the user's role is to evaluate and integrate these alternatives, maintaining responsibility for judgement and choice.

It is important to note that requesting alternatives does not imply relativism or indecision. The goal is not to avoid commitment, but to make commitment more informed. Effective communication involves moving between divergence and convergence—expanding the space of possibilities and then narrowing it deliberately. Metacommunication enables this movement by making shifts in strategy explicit.

Finally, the ability to request alternative approaches reflects an advanced level of AI communication literacy. It demonstrates awareness of the interpretive nature of AI output and a willingness to engage critically rather than accept responses at face value. By integrating this practice into regular interaction, users strengthen both the reliability and the intellectual value of human–AI dialogue.

This section highlights how metacommunication enables users to shape not only the form but the epistemic quality of AI interaction. The following section builds on this insight by examining reflective practices that allow users to evaluate and learn from their dialogue with AI over time (Fig. 7.3).

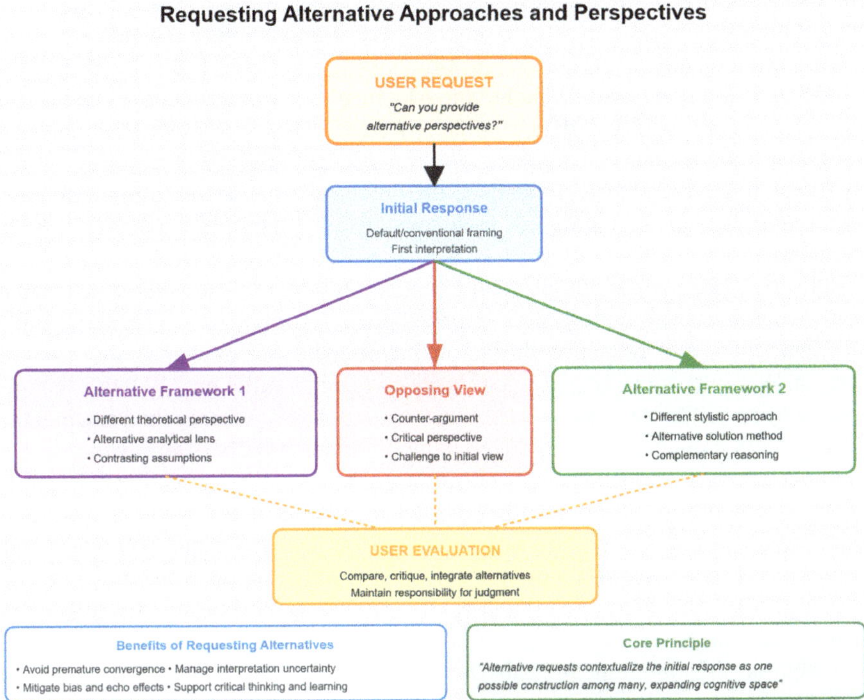

Fig. 7.3 Requesting alternative approaches and perspectives. This diagram illustrates the process of requesting alternative approaches and perspectives to expand cognitive space and avoid premature convergence in AI-assisted dialogue. Beginning with a user request for alternative perspectives, the system generates an initial response representing a default or conventional framing. This then diverges into multiple alternatives: Alternative framework 1 (offering different theoretical perspectives and analytical lenses), an opposing view (presenting counter-arguments and critical challenges) and alternative framework 2 (suggesting different stylistic approaches and complementary reasoning). These alternatives converge at the user evaluation stage, where the human remains responsible for comparing, critiquing and integrating them. The diagram depicts four key benefits: avoiding premature convergence, managing interpretation uncertainty, mitigating bias and echo effects and supporting critical thinking and learning. The core principle emphasises that alternative requests contextualise initial responses as provisional constructions among many possibilities

7.4 Reflecting on and Evaluating AI Communication

Reflection and evaluation are essential components of mature human–AI communication. While generative AI systems can adapt dynamically to input, they do not learn from interaction in the way humans do unless explicitly designed to do so. By contrast, human users can and should learn from each interaction. Reflecting on AI communication enables users to assess not only the quality of output but also the effectiveness of their communicative strategies. This reflective practice transforms interaction from episodic use into a process of continuous improvement.

Evaluation in human–AI communication operates on multiple levels. At the most immediate level, users assess whether the AI's response meets functional needs: Is it relevant, accurate, usable and appropriately framed? However, metacommunicative evaluation goes further. It examines *why* a particular response was produced and *how* communicative choices influenced the outcome. This deeper evaluation helps users refine their understanding of how generative AI interprets language, context and intent.

Reflective practice begins with attention to alignment. Users can ask whether the AI's output corresponds to their intended goals, assumptions and criteria. When misalignment occurs, reflection shifts from blaming the system to analysing communication. Was intent clearly expressed? Were constraints sufficient? Was the dialogue strategy appropriate for the task? This analytical stance reinforces the principle that communication quality is co-produced rather than unilaterally determined.

Another critical dimension of reflection concerns trust calibration. Users can reflect on how much confidence they placed in AI output and whether that confidence was justified. Over time, this practice helps develop more accurate mental models of AI capability and limitations. Reflection thus supports the dynamic calibration of trust discussed in earlier chapters, grounding it in experience rather than abstract caution.

Evaluating AI communication also involves ethical reflection. Users may consider whether AI assistance was appropriate for the task, whether outputs were integrated responsibly and whether human judgement was adequately exercised. In professional and educational contexts, such reflection supports integrity and accountability. Ethical evaluation is not an afterthought but part of communicative competence.

Reflection can be supported through explicit metacommunicative questions. Users may ask themselves what worked well in the interaction, what required correction and what could be communicated more effectively next time. These questions do not need to be formalised, but they benefit from consistency. Over time, patterns emerge that inform more effective communication strategies.

Importantly, reflective evaluation does not require perfection. Generative AI interaction is inherently uncertain and context-dependent. The goal of reflection is not to eliminate error but to understand it. By analysing misalignment and adjustment, users gain insight into both the system and their own communicative habits. This insight strengthens adaptability and resilience.

Reflection also contributes to learning transfer. Skills developed in one interaction can be applied to others when users abstract principles from experience. For example, recognising that certain types of ambiguity consistently lead to misinterpretation encourages more explicit framing in future tasks. Reflective practice thus accelerates the development of AI communication literacy.

Finally, reflecting on AI communication reinforces human agency. Rather than treating AI interaction as a black box, users engage with it as a communicative process subject to analysis and improvement. This stance aligns with the broader aims of the book: to position humans as intentional, responsible communicators in a world of increasingly capable AI systems.

Reflective evaluation prepares the ground for the final section of this chapter, which examines how metacommunication itself evolves as AI systems and communicative norms continue to change (Fig. 7.4).

7.5 Developing Metacommunicative Awareness Over Time

Metacommunicative awareness is not a fixed skill acquired through a single insight or technique; it develops gradually through sustained interaction, reflection and adaptation. As users engage repeatedly with generative AI systems, they accumulate experiential knowledge about how communication choices shape outcomes. Developing this awareness over time is essential for moving from competent interaction to genuinely fluent and reflective human–AI communication.

Early stages of AI use are often characterised by experimentation and occasional frustration. Users test what the system can do, encounter misalignment and adjust expectations. At this stage, metacommunication tends to be reactive: users correct misunderstandings after they occur. While valuable, this reactive mode limits learning to immediate problem-solving. Metacommunicative awareness deepens when users begin to anticipate communicative challenges and address them proactively through explicit framing, preference setting and strategy selection.

Over time, users develop a more nuanced mental model of AI behaviour. They recognise patterns in how ambiguity, constraints, tone and dialogue structure influence responses. This recognition enables them to choose communicative strategies deliberately rather than intuitively. For example, experienced users may anticipate when a task requires iterative refinement or when alternative perspectives should be requested from the outset. Such anticipatory communication reflects advanced metacommunicative competence.

Developing awareness also involves increased self-reflection. Users become more conscious of their own communicative habits, assumptions and preferences. They learn which interaction styles yield productive outcomes and which lead to friction. This self-awareness transforms AI communication into a reflective practice, similar to how experienced communicators adapt their style when working with different human interlocutors. The difference lies in the need to explicitly externalise these adaptations.

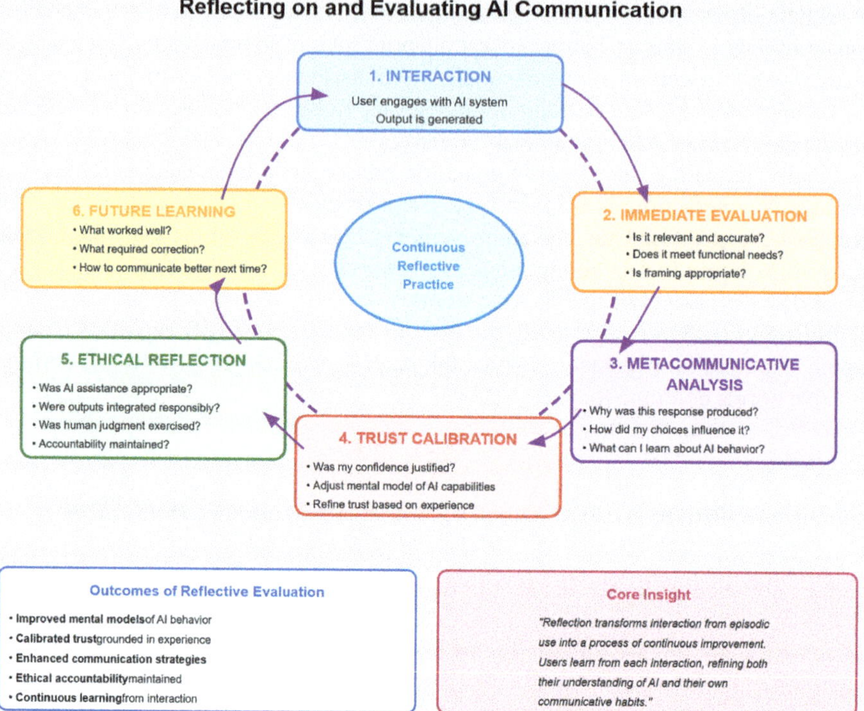

Fig. 7.4 Reflecting on and evaluating AI communication. This diagram depicts the cyclical process of reflecting on and evaluating AI communication as a continuous practice for developing mature human–AI interaction competence. The reflective cycle encompasses six interconnected stages: (1) Interaction, where users engage with the AI system and output is generated; (2) immediate evaluation, assessing relevance, accuracy and functional adequacy; (3) metacommunicative analysis, examining why responses were produced and how communicative choices influenced outcomes; (4) trust calibration, adjusting confidence levels and mental models based on experience; (5) ethical reflection, considering appropriateness, responsible integration and human judgement; and (6) future learning, identifying what worked, what required correction and strategies for improvement. The diagram illustrates five key outcomes: improved mental models of AI behaviour, calibrated trust grounded in experience, enhanced communication strategies, maintained ethical accountability and continuous learning from interaction. This reflective practice transforms episodic use into systematic improvement

Metacommunicative awareness is reinforced through comparison across contexts. As users apply AI communication skills in diverse domains—education, research, professional work or creative practice—they observe how communicative strategies transfer and where they require adaptation. This cross-contextual learning strengthens flexibility and prevents rigid reliance on a single interaction pattern.

Importantly, developing metacommunicative awareness also involves recognising the evolving nature of AI systems. Generative models change over time in capability, modality and interface. Users who cultivate reflective communication habits are better equipped to adapt to these changes. Rather than relying on memorised techniques, they focus on principles and communicative sensitivity. This adaptability ensures that AI communication literacy remains relevant despite technological evolution.

There is also a social dimension to metacommunicative development. As AI becomes embedded in collective practices, communication norms emerge and evolve. Users who reflect on their interactions help shape these norms—through teaching, collaboration and example. Metacommunicative awareness thus extends beyond individual competence to collective understanding of how humans and AI should communicate.

Finally, developing metacommunicative awareness reinforces the central theme of this book: communication with generative AI is a human skill. It is learned, refined and contextualised through practice. AI systems may generate language, but humans generate meaning by framing interaction, evaluating output and reflecting on the process. Metacommunication makes this meaning-making explicit.

By cultivating awareness over time, users transform AI interaction from a series of isolated exchanges into an evolving communicative relationship. This transformation enables more effective collaboration, more responsible use and deeper insight into both human and artificial communication. This chapter thus completes the book's conceptual arc by showing how communication competence extends beyond techniques and principles into reflective mastery (Fig. 7.5).

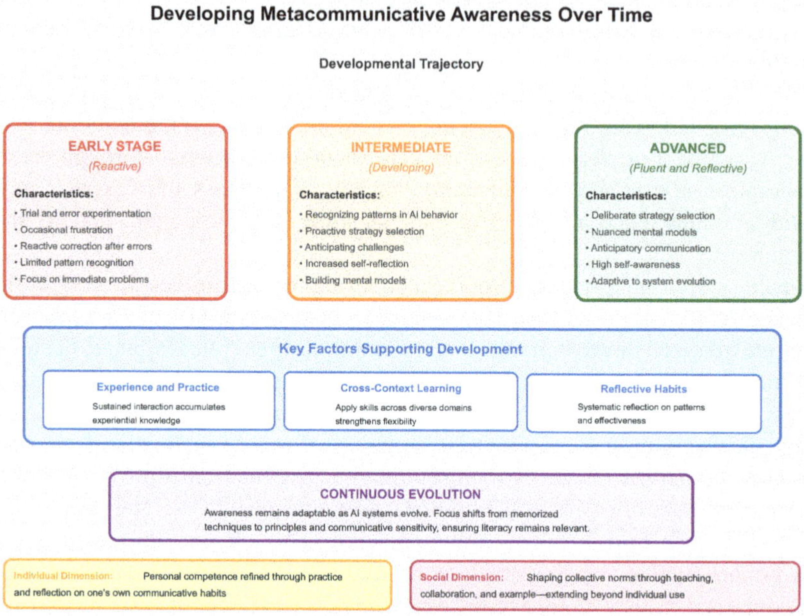

Fig. 7.5 Developing metacommunicative awareness over time. This diagram shows the developmental trajectory of metacommunicative awareness as users progress from reactive novices to fluent, reflective communicators. The gradient timeline depicts three developmental stages: early stage (reactive), characterised by trial-and-error experimentation, occasional frustration, reactive correction, limited pattern recognition and focus on immediate problems; intermediate stage (developing), marked by recognising patterns in AI behaviour, proactive strategy selection, anticipating challenges, increased self-reflection and building mental models; and advanced stage (fluent and reflective), distinguished by deliberate strategy selection, nuanced mental models, anticipatory communication, high self-awareness and adaptability to system evolution. Three key factors support development: sustained experience and practice that accumulate experiential knowledge, cross-context learning that strengthens flexibility across diverse domains and reflective habits that involve systematic evaluation of patterns and effectiveness. The diagram emphasises continuous evolution, with both individual and social dimensions shaping collective norms

Bibliography

1. Amershi, S., Cakmak, M., Knox, W.B., Kulesza, T.: Power to the people: The role of humans in interactive machine learning. AI Mag. **35**(4), 105–120 (2014). https://doi.org/10.1609/aimag.v35i4.2513
2. Bansal, G., Wu, T., Zhou, J., et al.: Does the whole exceed its parts? The effect of AI explanations on complementary team performance. In: Proceedings of the 2021 CHI Conference on Human Factors in Computing Systems, pp. 1–16. ACM, New York (2021). https://doi.org/10.1145/3411764.3445717
3. Bateson, G.: Steps to an Ecology of Mind: Collected Essays in Anthropology, Psychiatry, Evolution, and Epistemology. University of Chicago Press, Chicago (1972)

4. Bødker, S.: When second wave HCI meets third wave challenges. In: Proceedings of the 4th Nordic Conference on Human-Computer Interaction, pp. 1–8. ACM, New York (2006). https://doi.org/10.1145/1182475.1182476

5. Bown, J., White, E., Boopalan, A.: Looking for the ultimate display: A brief history of social VR. In: Cranford, J., Srinivasan, R., Lu, Y. (eds.) Virtual, Augmented, and Mixed Realities in Education, pp. 1–18. Springer, Singapore (2021). https://doi.org/10.1007/978-981-15-9329-9_1

6. Buccinca, Z., Cheng, J.Y., Gajos, K.Z.: Who should decide what AI can do? Policies for training data selection and their implications for fairness. Proc. ACM Hum.-Comput. Interact. 7(CSCW2), 1–25 (2023). https://doi.org/10.1145/3610066

7. Buçinca, Z., Lin, P., Gajos, K.Z., Glassman, E.L.: Proxy tasks and subjective measures can be misleading in evaluating explainable AI systems. In: Proceedings of the 25th International Conference on Intelligent User Interfaces, pp. 454–464. ACM, New York (2020). https://doi.org/10.1145/3377325.3377498

8. Chandrasekaran, B., Josephson, J.R., Benjamins, V.R.: What are ontologies, and why do we need them? IEEE Intell. Syst. Appl. 14(1), 20–26 (1999). https://doi.org/10.1109/5254.747902

9. Clark, H.H., Schaefer, E.F.: Contributing to discourse. Cogn. Sci. 13(2), 259–294 (1989). https://doi.org/10.1207/s15516709cog1302_7

10. Collins, H.: Tacit and Explicit Knowledge. University of Chicago Press, Chicago (2010)

11. Cummings, M.L.: Automation bias in intelligent time critical decision support systems. In: AIAA 1st Intelligent Systems Technical Conference, pp. 1–6. American Institute of Aeronautics and Astronautics, Reston (2004). https://doi.org/10.2514/6.2004-6313

12. Dreyfus, H.L., Dreyfus, S.E.: Mind Over Machine: The Power of Human Intuition and Expertise in the Era of the Computer. Free Press, New York (1986)

13. Dweck, C.S.: Mindset: The New Psychology of Success. Random House, New York (2006)

14. Ericsson, K.A.: Deliberate practice and acquisition of expert performance: A general overview. Acad. Emerg. Med. 15(11), 988–994 (2008). https://doi.org/10.1111/j.1553-2712.2008.00227.x

15. Geroimenko, V.: The Essential Guide to Prompt Engineering: Key Principles, Techniques, Challenges, and Security Risks, Springer, Cham (2025)

16. Geroimenko, V.: Beyond and After Prompt Engineering: The Future of AI Communication, Springer, Cham (2026)

17. Geroimenko, V. (ed.): Human-Computer Creativity: Generative AI in Education, Art, and Healthcare, Springer, Cham (2025)

18. Kolb, D.A.: Experiential Learning: Experience as the Source of Learning and Development, 2nd edn. Pearson Education, Upper Saddle River (2015)

19. Kulesza, T., Burnett, M., Wong, W.-K., Stumpf, S.: Principles of explanatory debugging to personalize interactive machine learning. In: Proceedings of the 20th International Conference on Intelligent User Interfaces, pp. 126–137. ACM, New York (2015). https://doi.org/10.1145/2678025.2701399

20. Lee, J.D., See, K.A.: Trust in automation: Designing for appropriate reliance. Hum. Factors 46(1), 50–80 (2004). https://doi.org/10.1518/hfes.46.1.50.30392

21. Mackay, W.E.: Responding to cognitive overload: Co-adaptive interface design. In: Diaper, D., Sasse, A. (eds.) Human-Computer Interaction—INTERACT'90, pp. 1023–1027. North-Holland, Amsterdam (1990)

22. Norman, D.A.: The Design of Everyday Things: Revised and Expanded Edition. Basic Books, New York (2013)

23. Nunes, I., Jannach, D.: A systematic review and taxonomy of explanations in decision support and recommender systems. User Model. User-Adapt. Interact. 27(3), 393–444 (2017). https://doi.org/10.1007/s11257-017-9195-0

24. Riedl, M.O.: Human-centered artificial intelligence and machine learning. Hum. Behav. Emerg. Technol. 1(1), 33–36 (2019). https://doi.org/10.1002/hbe2.117

25. Schön, D.A.: The Reflective Practitioner: How Professionals Think in Action. Basic Books, New York (1983)

26. Seeber, I., Bittner, E., Briggs, R.O., et al.: Machines as teammates: A research agenda on AI in team collaboration. Inf. Manag. **57**(2), 103174 (2020). https://doi.org/10.1016/j.im.2019.103174

27. Shneiderman, B.: Bridging the Gap Between Ethics and Practice: Guidelines for Reliable, Safe, and Trustworthy Human-Centered AI Systems. ACM Trans. Interact. Intell. Syst. **10**(4), 1–31 (2020). https://doi.org/10.1145/3419764

28. Suchman, L.A.: Plans and Situated Actions: The Problem of Human-Machine Communication. Cambridge University Press, Cambridge (1987)

29. Watzlawick, P., Bavelas, J.B., Jackson, D.D.: Pragmatics of Human Communication: A Study of Interactional Patterns, Pathologies, and Paradoxes. W. W. Norton, New York (1967)

30. Winograd, T., Flores, F.: Understanding Computers and Cognition: A New Foundation for Design. Ablex, Norwood (1986)

31. Yang, Q., Steinfeld, A., Rosé, C., Zimmerman, J.: Re-examining whether, why, and how human-AI interaction is uniquely difficult to design. In: Proceedings of the 2020 CHI Conference on Human Factors in Computing Systems, pp. 1–13. ACM, New York (2020). https://doi.org/10.1145/3313831.3376301

32. Zhang, Y., Liao, Q.V., Bellamy, R.K.E.: Effect of confidence and explanation on accuracy and trust calibration in AI-assisted decision making. In: Proceedings of the 2020 Conference on Fairness, Accountability, and Transparency, pp. 295–305. ACM, New York (2020). https://doi.org/10.1145/3351095.3372852

33. Zimmerman, J., Forlizzi, J., Evenson, S.: Research through design as a method for interaction design research in HCI. In: Proceedings of the SIGCHI Conference on Human Factors in Computing Systems, pp. 493–502. ACM, New York (2007). https://doi.org/10.1145/1240624.1240704

Chapter 8
The Future Perspective of Human–AI Communication

This final chapter draws together the conceptual, practical and ethical threads developed throughout the book to reflect on the future of human–AI communication. As generative AI systems continue to evolve in capability and reach, the challenge facing humans is not merely how to use these systems, but how to communicate with them in ways that are intentional, adaptive and responsible. This chapter reframes effective AI interaction as a form of communication literacy that transcends specific tools or techniques. By examining adaptability, societal and educational implications and the enduring human role in shaping communicative norms, the chapter offers a forward-looking perspective on how humans can engage with generative AI as communicative partners while retaining agency, judgement and accountability.

8.1 From Prompting to Communication Literacy

The rapid adoption of generative AI has brought unprecedented attention to the act of 'prompting' as a means of interacting with intelligent systems. Early discussions understandably focused on how to phrase inputs effectively in order to obtain useful outputs. However, as this book has argued throughout, prompting represents only an initial and partial framing of a much broader phenomenon. What is emerging is not merely a new technical skill, but a new form of communication literacy—one that requires humans to engage with AI systems reflectively, strategically and responsibly.

In its narrow sense, prompting treats interaction as a one-way instruction: the user issues a request and the system responds. While this model can be effective for simple tasks, it quickly reaches its limits in complex, iterative or high-stakes contexts. Generative AI systems interpret language probabilistically and contextually, not deterministically. As a result, meaningful interaction depends less on isolated phrasing of prompts and more on how dialogue is framed, maintained, evaluated and adapted over time. Communication literacy encompasses this broader skill set.

V. Geroimenko, *Communication Skills for Generative AI*, Human–Computer Interaction Series, https://doi.org/10.1007/978-3-032-21689-2_8

Communication literacy with AI involves understanding how meaning is co-constructed through interaction. It requires awareness of how context, intent, constraints, tone and iteration shape AI responses. It also involves recognising the limits of AI understanding and the need for human judgement at every stage. Unlike traditional digital literacy, which often focuses on tool use and interface navigation, AI communication literacy is dialogical and reflective. It treats interaction as an evolving process rather than a discrete command.

This shift has important implications for how humans conceptualise their role in AI-mediated environments. When interaction is reduced to prompting, responsibility appears diffuse: the system produces output and the user reacts. When interaction is understood as communication, responsibility becomes explicit. Users must consider how their framing influences outcomes, how their trust is calibrated and how AI contributions are integrated into human decision-making. Communication literacy, therefore, reinforces human agency rather than diminishing it.

Another defining feature of AI communication literacy is transferability. Prompting techniques are often tied to specific models or interfaces and may become obsolete as systems evolve. Communicative principles, by contrast, are adaptable. Skills such as clarifying intent, managing ambiguity, negotiating roles and reflecting on dialogue remain relevant across platforms, modalities and future generations of AI systems. This durability makes communication literacy a more robust foundation for long-term human–AI interaction.

Education and professional practice will increasingly depend on this broader literacy. In educational settings, students must learn not only how to obtain answers from AI but also how to engage critically, reflectively and ethically with AI-supported dialogue. In professional contexts, effective communication with AI becomes a prerequisite for reliable analysis, creative collaboration and responsible decision support. Treating AI communication as a literacy foregrounds learning, practice and reflection rather than optimisation tricks.

Finally, moving from prompting to communication literacy changes how success is evaluated. The goal is no longer to produce the 'perfect prompt', but to sustain productive, aligned and ethically grounded interaction over time. Misunderstandings are not failures but opportunities for refinement. Dialogue becomes a space for learning, negotiation and co-creation rather than mere execution.

This reframing marks a critical step in the maturation of human–AI interaction. As generative AI becomes more capable and more deeply embedded in human activity, the ability to communicate effectively with such systems will be as fundamental as writing, reasoning or collaboration. The following section extends this perspective by examining how communication literacy supports adaptability to rapidly evolving AI technologies (Fig. 8.1).

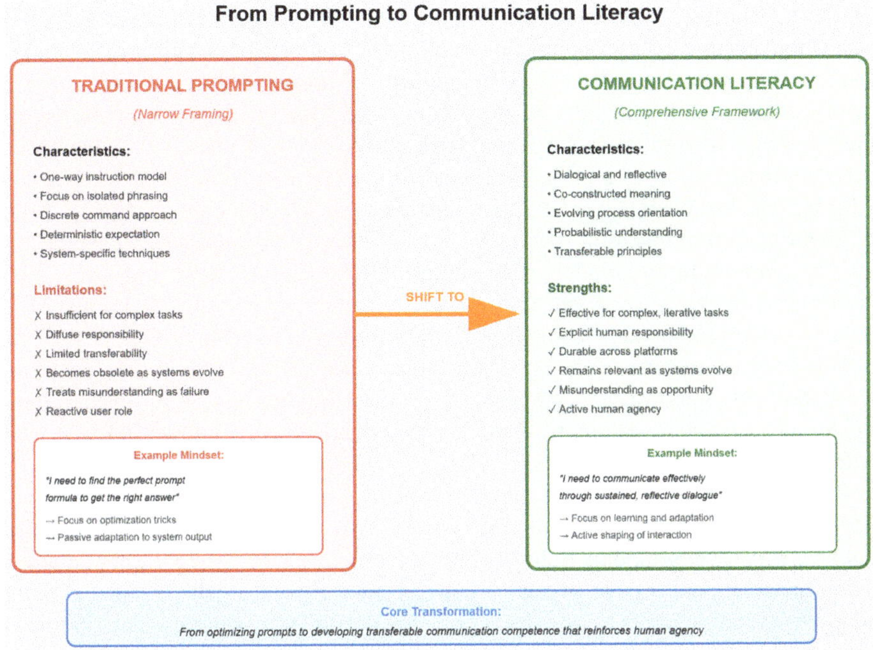

Fig. 8.1 From prompting to communication literacy. This diagram illustrates the fundamental shift from traditional prompting to comprehensive communication literacy in human–AI interaction. The left panel depicts traditional prompting as a narrow framing characterised by one-way instruction, isolated phrasing, discrete commands and deterministic expectations, with system-specific techniques that become obsolete and foster diffuse responsibility. This approach proves insufficient for complex tasks and positions users reactively. The right panel presents communication literacy as a comprehensive framework that emphasises dialogical, reflective engagement, where meaning is co-constructed through evolving processes that acknowledge probabilistic AI interpretation. This approach employs transferable principles that remain durable across platforms, explicitly reinforces human responsibility and agency and transforms misunderstandings into learning opportunities. The core transformation moves from optimising prompts to developing transferable communication competence, marking critical maturation in how humans conceptualise their role in AI-mediated environments and supporting long-term effective collaboration

8.2 Adapting Communication Practices to Evolving AI Systems

Generative AI systems are evolving at a pace that challenges traditional models of skill acquisition and expertise. New capabilities, modalities and interaction paradigms are introduced continuously, reshaping how humans engage with intelligent systems. In this context, effective human–AI communication cannot rely on static techniques or fixed assumptions. Instead, it requires adaptive communication practices grounded in enduring principles rather than transient features.

One of the key challenges posed by evolving AI systems is the instability of interaction norms. As models gain new capabilities—such as multimodal understanding, longer contextual memory or real-time responsiveness—previous communicative strategies may become insufficient or suboptimal. Users who rely on memorised prompts or rigid workflows may struggle to adapt, while those who understand communication at a principled level can adjust their practices more fluidly. Adaptability thus becomes a defining element of AI communication literacy.

Adapting communication practices begins with recognising that AI systems are not uniform. Different models may interpret language, context and constraints in subtly different ways. Even updates to the same system can alter interaction dynamics. Communicative competence, therefore, involves attentiveness to feedback and responsiveness to change. Users must observe how AI behaviour shifts and adjust framing, iteration and metacommunication accordingly. This observational sensitivity mirrors how humans adapt communication when interacting with new collaborators or cultural contexts.

Another aspect of adaptation concerns modality expansion. As AI systems increasingly integrate text, images, audio and other forms of interaction, communication practices must accommodate richer and more complex exchanges. Multimodal interaction amplifies expressive potential but also increases the risk of misalignment. Adaptive communicators learn to intentionally coordinate modalities, clarifying how different inputs relate and which elements carry primary meaning. This requires not only technical familiarity but communicative awareness.

Adaptation also involves recalibrating expectations. As AI systems become more capable in some areas, users may be tempted to assume broader competence. Conversely, awareness of persistent limitations may lead to undue scepticism. Effective communication practices incorporate continuous trust calibration, adjusting reliance based on observed performance rather than static beliefs. This dynamic calibration supports responsible use and mitigates both overconfidence and underutilisation.

Importantly, adapting communication practices does not mean abandoning ethical and reflective standards in favour of efficiency. On the contrary, rapid technological change heightens the importance of deliberate communication. As AI systems influence more decisions and creative processes, the consequences of miscommunication increase. Adaptive communication, therefore, includes maintaining transparency, accountability and critical evaluation even as interaction becomes more seamless.

Educational and organisational contexts play a crucial role in fostering adaptive communication. Teaching users to reflect on interaction patterns, experiment with dialogue strategies and articulate communicative intent equips them to navigate technological change. Rather than training users on specific systems, education should focus on transferable communication skills that remain relevant as systems evolve.

Finally, adaptation underscores the reciprocal nature of human–AI communication. While AI systems adapt algorithmically, humans adapt communicatively. The quality of interaction emerges from this interplay. Users who cultivate adaptive communication practices are better positioned to harness new capabilities without being destabilised by change.

This adaptive perspective reinforces the book's central argument: effective communication with generative AI is not about mastering a particular tool but about developing communicative resilience. The following section extends this argument by examining the broader societal and cultural implications of widespread AI communication literacy (Fig. 8.2).

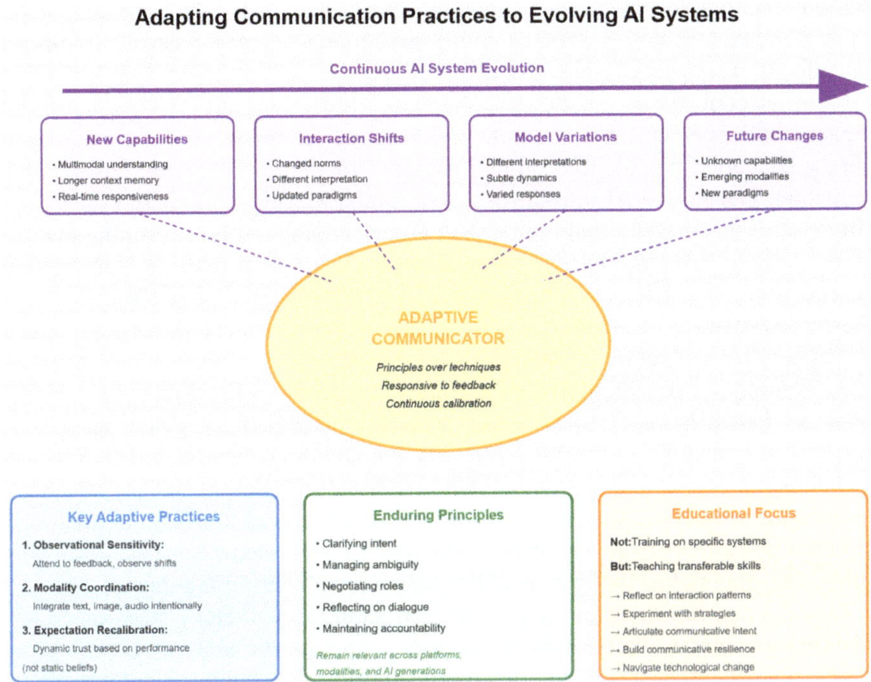

Fig. 8.2 Adapting communication practices to evolving AI systems. This diagram depicts the relationship between continuously evolving AI systems and the adaptive communicator who navigates technological change through enduring communicative principles. Along the top, four categories of AI evolution are illustrated: new capabilities (multimodal understanding, more extended context memory, real-time responsiveness), interaction shifts (changed norms and paradigms), model variations (different interpretations and dynamics) and future changes (unknown capabilities and emerging modalities). At the centre, the adaptive communicator employs principles over techniques, remains responsive to feedback and practices continuous calibration. Three key adaptive practices are highlighted: observational sensitivity to feedback and behavioural shifts, modality coordination integrating text, image and audio intentionally and expectation recalibration based on dynamic performance assessment rather than static beliefs. The diagram emphasises enduring principles—clarifying intent, managing ambiguity, negotiating roles, reflecting on dialogue and maintaining accountability—that remain relevant across all AI generations, alongside educational focus on transferable skills

8.3 Societal and Educational Implications of AI Communication Literacy

The emergence of generative AI as a pervasive communicative technology has implications that extend well beyond individual interaction practices. As AI systems become embedded in education, professional work, governance and everyday life, the ability to communicate effectively with them becomes a societal competence rather than a niche technical skill. AI communication literacy, therefore, carries significant educational, institutional and cultural consequences.

From an educational perspective, the shift from prompting to communication literacy challenges existing curricula and pedagogical models. Traditional digital literacy education has focused on tool use, information retrieval and basic critical evaluation. Generative AI introduces a new dimension: dialogue-based interaction with systems that produce language, reasoning and creative output. Teaching students merely how to 'use' AI systems is insufficient. They must learn to frame intent, manage ambiguity, reflect on dialogue and critically evaluate AI-generated content. These competencies align more closely with communication, reasoning and ethical judgement than with conventional technical training.

AI communication literacy also reshapes educators' roles. Rather than acting solely as gatekeepers of information, educators increasingly guide students in engaging responsibly and reflectively with AI-supported dialogue. This includes modelling effective communication practices, discussing limitations and biases and encouraging metacognitive awareness of how AI influences thinking. In this sense, AI communication literacy supports educational goals related to critical thinking, authorship and intellectual responsibility rather than undermining them.

At a societal level, disparities in AI communication literacy may exacerbate existing inequalities. Individuals and groups who lack the skills to communicate effectively with AI systems may be disadvantaged in education, employment and access to information. Conversely, those who develop advanced communicative competence can leverage AI more effectively for learning, creativity and decision-making. Addressing this gap requires viewing AI communication literacy as a public good rather than a specialist expertise.

Organisations and institutions also face new challenges. As AI-mediated communication becomes routine, norms around authorship, accountability and transparency must be renegotiated. Policies that focus exclusively on regulating AI technology without addressing human communicative practice risk being ineffective. Institutional frameworks should therefore incorporate guidance on responsible AI communication, including expectations around disclosure, verification and human oversight.

Culturally, the widespread adoption of generative AI invites reflection on how meaning is produced and shared. Language has long been a distinctly human medium for reasoning, creativity and social coordination. When AI systems participate in linguistic production, communication practices acquire new layers of mediation. AI communication literacy enables societies to engage with this shift thoughtfully rather than reactively, preserving human values while embracing technological support.

There are also implications for democratic discourse and public communication. Generative AI can amplify voices, generate persuasive content and influence opinion. Without widespread communication literacy, these capabilities may be misused or misunderstood. Educating citizens to recognise AI-mediated communication, question its sources and evaluate its intent becomes essential for maintaining informed public discourse.

Finally, the societal impact of AI communication literacy underscores the importance of interdisciplinary collaboration. Addressing these challenges requires insights from education, communication studies, ethics, psychology and computer science. By framing AI interaction as a communicative practice rather than a technical problem, this book contributes to a broader conversation about how societies adapt to intelligent systems.

The final section of this chapter draws these threads together by returning to the human role in shaping the future of AI communication and collaboration (Fig. 8.3).

8.4 The Human Role in Shaping the Future of AI Communication

As generative AI systems become increasingly capable and widespread, the future of human–AI communication will not be determined by technology alone. It will be shaped decisively by human choices: how people communicate with AI, how they integrate AI into social and institutional practices and how they define responsibility and agency within AI-mediated interaction. This book has argued consistently that communication is the primary site where this future is negotiated.

Generative AI does not introduce meaning, values or goals into interaction. It responds to communicative input within the constraints of its design and training. Humans, therefore, remain the architects of communicative intent. The quality, direction and consequences of AI communication depend on how humans frame dialogue, evaluate output and reflect on interaction. In this sense, the future of AI communication is inseparable from the future of human communicative competence.

One of the central risks in the evolving AI landscape is the erosion of human agency through unreflective use. As AI systems become more fluent, responsive and integrated into workflows, it may become tempting to defer judgement, outsource reasoning, or accept AI-generated content as authoritative. Such tendencies do not arise from AI capability itself, but from communicative habits that minimise reflection and responsibility. The human role in shaping the future of AI communication, therefore, involves resisting passive interaction and cultivating deliberate, reflective engagement.

Societal and Educational Implications of AI Communication Literacy

AI COMMUNICATION LITERACY

A societal competence, not a niche technical skill
Essential for education, work, governance, and daily life

EDUCATIONAL IMPLICATIONS

Curriculum Transformation:

- Beyond tool use to dialogue-based interaction
- Frame intent, manage ambiguity, reflect on dialogue
- Critical evaluation of AI-generated content

Educator Roles:

- Guide responsible AI engagement
- Model effective communication practices
- Discuss limitations and biases
- Encourage metacognitive awareness

EQUITY and ACCESS IMPLICATIONS

Risk of Disparity:

- Lack of literacy → disadvantage in education, employment, information access
- Advanced competence → leverage for learning, creativity, decision-making

Critical Response:

- View AI literacy as a public good
- Ensure inclusive access to education
- Prevent exacerbation of inequalities

INSTITUTIONAL IMPLICATIONS

Renegotiating Norms:

- Authorship standards
- Accountability frameworks
- Transparency expectations

Policy Requirements:

- Guidance on responsible AI communication
- Disclosure expectations
- Verification requirements
- Human oversight mandates

Focus on communicative practice, not just technology regulation

CULTURAL and DEMOCRATIC IMPLICATIONS

Meaning Production:

- Language as mediated human practice
- New layers of meaning-making
- Thoughtful engagement with shift

Democratic Discourse:

- Recognize AI-mediated communication
- Question sources and intent
- Evaluate AI influence on opinion
- Maintain informed public discourse

Essential for democratic participation

Requires interdisciplinary collaboration: education, communication studies, ethics, psychology, computer science

Fig. 8.3 Societal and educational implications of AI communication literacy. This diagram shows the broad societal and educational implications of AI communication literacy as a fundamental societal competence essential for education, work, governance and daily life. The diagram presents four interconnected implication domains: Educational implications address curriculum transformation beyond tool use towards dialogue-based interaction, framing intent, managing ambiguity and critical evaluation, while educators guide responsible engagement and model effective practices. Equity and access implications highlight risks of disparity, where literacy gaps disadvantage individuals in education and employment and require treating AI literacy as a public good with inclusive access. Institutional implications necessitate renegotiating norms around authorship, accountability and transparency, requiring policies focused on communicative practice rather than solely technology regulation. Cultural and democratic implications recognise language as a mediated human practice with new layers of meaning-making, requiring citizens to recognise AI-mediated communication and evaluate its influence to maintain informed public discourse. The diagram emphasises interdisciplinary collaboration across education, communication studies, ethics, psychology and computer science

Equally important is the role of humans in setting norms. Communication practices become normalised through repetition, imitation and institutional reinforcement. If AI interaction is treated primarily as command execution or answer retrieval, these norms will shape future systems and expectations. If, by contrast, AI communication is framed as dialogue, collaboration and shared meaning-making, different norms will emerge. Humans influence this trajectory through everyday communicative choices as well as through education, policy and professional standards.

Human responsibility also extends to ethical stewardship. Generative AI systems reflect and amplify patterns present in their training data and usage contexts. Communicative practices that challenge bias, request transparency and encourage reflection help counteract these tendencies. Ethical AI communication is not achieved solely through regulation or technical safeguards; it is enacted continuously through how humans communicate with and about AI.

Another crucial aspect of the human role lies in adaptation. AI systems will continue to change in capability and form, but human communicative principles provide continuity. By focusing on communication literacy rather than system-specific techniques, humans can remain adaptable without becoming dependent on particular technologies. This adaptability ensures that human values remain central even as technical affordances evolve.

The future of AI communication will also be collective. As AI becomes embedded in shared environments—classrooms, workplaces, public discourse—the consequences of communication practices extend beyond individual users. Humans shape not only their own interactions, but the communicative ecology in which others participate. Recognising this collective dimension reinforces the importance of inclusive education, transparent norms and shared responsibility.

Ultimately, this book has advanced a far-reaching but straightforward claim: generative AI changes what machines can do with language, but it does not alter what humans must do with communication. Humans must still articulate intent, interpret meaning, evaluate reliability and assume responsibility for action. AI communication does not diminish these roles; it intensifies them.

By approaching generative AI as a communicative partner rather than an autonomous authority, humans retain their central role in shaping interaction. The future of AI communication is therefore not a technological destiny, but a communicative choice—one that depends on the skills, values and awareness humans bring to dialogue with intelligent systems (Fig. 8.4).

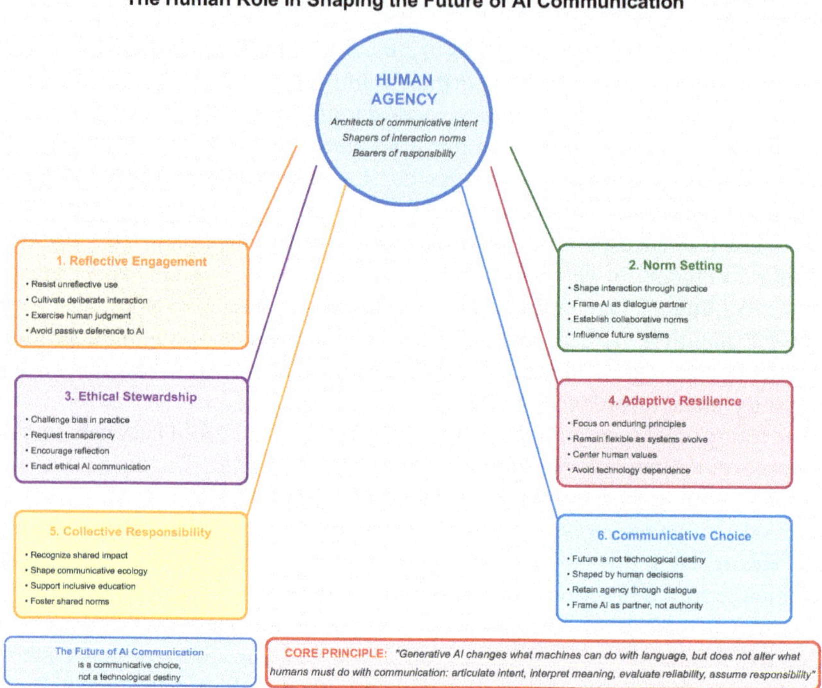

Fig. 8.4   The human role in shaping the future of AI communication. This diagram explains the decisive human role in shaping the future of AI communication through six interconnected dimensions radiating from central human agency as architects of communicative intent, shapers of interaction norms and bearers of responsibility. The six key roles include: (1) Reflective engagement—resisting unreflective use, cultivating deliberate interaction, exercising judgement and avoiding passive deference; (2) norm setting—shaping interaction through practice, framing AI as dialogue partner, establishing collaborative norms and influencing future systems; (3) Ethical Stewardship—challenging bias, requesting transparency, encouraging reflection and enacting ethical communication continuously; (4) adaptive resilience—focusing on enduring principles, remaining flexible as systems evolve, centring human values and avoiding technology dependence; (5) collective responsibility—recognising shared impact, shaping communicative ecology, supporting inclusive education and fostering shared norms; and (6) communicative choice—recognising the future as shaped by human decisions rather than technological destiny. The diagram emphasises the core principle that while AI changes what machines can do with language, humans must still articulate intent, interpret meaning, evaluate reliability and assume responsibility

Bibliography

1. Bardzell, J., Bardzell, S.: Humanistic HCI. Interactions 23(2), 20–23 (2016). https://doi.org/10.1145/2888576
2. Bawden, D., Robinson, L.: The dark side of information: overload, anxiety and other paradoxes and pathologies. J. Inf. Sci. 35(2), 180–191 (2009). https://doi.org/10.1177/0165551508095781
3. Bender, E.M., Gebru, T., McMillan-Major, A., Shmitchell, S.: On the dangers of stochastic parrots: Can language models be too big? In: Proceedings of the 2021 ACM Conference on

Fairness, Accountability, and Transparency, pp. 610–623. ACM, New York (2021). https://doi.org/10.1145/3442188.3445922
4. Birhane, A., Kalluri, P., Card, D., et al.: The values encoded in machine learning research. In: Proceedings of the 2022 ACM Conference on Fairness, Accountability, and Transparency, pp. 173–184. ACM, New York (2022). https://doi.org/10.1145/3531146.3533083
5. Brynjolfsson, E., Mitchell, T.: What can machine learning do? Workforce implications. Science 358(6370), 1530–1534 (2017). https://doi.org/10.1126/science.aap8062
6. Buckingham, D.: Defining digital literacy: What do young people need to know about digital media? Nord. J. Digit. Lit. 2006(1), 263–276 (2006)
7. Cardon, P.W., Fleischmann, C., Aritz, J., et al.: The challenges and opportunities of communicating with algorithms. Bus. Prof. Commun. Q. 86(3), 272–302 (2023). https://doi.org/10.1177/23294906231181558
8. Crawford, K.: Atlas of AI: Power, Politics, and the Planetary Costs of Artificial Intelligence. Yale University Press, New Haven (2021)
9. Daugherty, P.R., Wilson, H.J.: Human + Machine: Reimagining Work in the Age of AI. Harvard Business Review Press, Boston (2018)
10. Diakopoulos, N.: Accountability in algorithmic decision making. Commun. ACM 59(2), 56–62 (2016). https://doi.org/10.1145/2844110
11. Eglash, R., Bennett, A., O'Donnell, C., et al.: Culturally situated design tools: Ethnocomputing from field site to classroom. Am. Anthropol. 108(2), 347–362 (2006). https://doi.org/10.1525/aa.2006.108.2.347
12. Eshet-Alkalai, Y.: Digital literacy: A conceptual framework for survival skills in the digital era. J. Educ. Multimed. Hypermedia 13(1), 93–106 (2004)
13. Eurbanks, V.: Automating Inequality: How High-Tech Tools Profile, Police, and Punish the Poor. St. Martin's Press, New York (2018)
14. Fazelpour, S., Danks, D.: Algorithmic bias: Senses, sources, solutions. Philos. Compass 16(8), e12760 (2021). https://doi.org/10.1111/phc3.12760
15. Floridi, L., Cowls, J., Beltrametti, M., et al.: AI4People—An ethical framework for a good AI society: Opportunities, risks, principles, and recommendations. Minds Mach. 28(4), 689–707 (2018). https://doi.org/10.1007/s11023-018-9482-5
16. Freire, P.: Pedagogy of the Oppressed, 30th Anniversary edn. Continuum, New York (2000)
17. Geroimenko, V.: The Essential Guide to Prompt Engineering: Key Principles, Techniques, Challenges, and Security Risks, Springer, Cham (2025)
18. Geroimenko, V.: Beyond and After Prompt Engineering: The Future of AI Communication, Springer, Cham (2026)
19. Geroimenko, V. (ed.): Human-Computer Creativity: Generative AI in Education, Art, and Healthcare, Springer, Cham (2025)
20. Green, B.: The Flaws of Policies Requiring Human Oversight of Government Algorithms. Comput. Law Secur. Rev. 45, 105681 (2022). https://doi.org/10.1016/j.clsr.2022.105681
21. Haraway, D.J.: Simians, Cyborgs, and Women: The Reinvention of Nature. Routledge, New York (1991)
22. Holstein, K., Vaughan, J.W.: Designing accountable systems. In: Proceedings of the 2022 ACM Conference on Fairness, Accountability, and Transparency, pp. 1887–1889. ACM, New York (2022). https://doi.org/10.1145/3531146.3533236
23. Iivari, N., Sharma, S., Ventä-Olkkonen, L.: Digital transformation of everyday life – How COVID-19 pandemic transformed the basic education of the young generation and why information management research should care? Int. J. Inf. Manag. 55, 102183 (2020). https://doi.org/10.1016/j.ijinfomgt.2020.102183
24. Jasanoff, S.: Technologies of Humility: Citizen Participation in Governing Science. Minerva 41(3), 223–244 (2003). https://doi.org/10.1023/A:1025557512320
25. Jobin, A., Ienca, M., Vayena, E.: The global landscape of AI ethics guidelines. Nat. Mach. Intell. 1(9), 389–399 (2019). https://doi.org/10.1038/s42256-019-0088-2
26. Long, D., Magerko, B.: What is AI literacy? Competencies and design considerations. In: Proceedings of the 2020 CHI Conference on Human Factors in Computing Systems, pp. 1–16. ACM, New York (2020). https://doi.org/10.1145/3313831.3376727

27. Mittelstadt, B.D., Allo, P., Taddeo, M., et al.: The ethics of algorithms: Mapping the debate. Big Data Soc. 3(2), 2053951716679679 (2016). https://doi.org/10.1177/2053951716679679
28. Noble, S.U.: Algorithms of Oppression: How Search Engines Reinforce Racism. New York University Press, New York (2018)
29. Rahwan, I., Cebrian, M., Obradovich, N., et al.: Machine behaviour. Nature 568(7753), 477–486 (2019). https://doi.org/10.1038/s41586-019-1138-y
30. Ribeiro, M.T., Wu, T., Guestrin, C., Singh, S.: Beyond accuracy: Behavioral testing of NLP models with CheckList. In: Proceedings of the 58th Annual Meeting of the Association for Computational Linguistics, pp. 4902–4912. Association for Computational Linguistics, Stroudsburg (2020). https://doi.org/10.18653/v1/2020.acl-main.442
31. Riedl, M.O., Harrison, B.: Using stories to teach human values to artificial agents. In: Proceedings of the 2nd International Workshop on AI, Ethics, and Society. AAAI Press, Palo Alto (2016)
32. Selwyn, N.: Education and Technology: Key Issues and Debates, 2nd edn. Bloomsbury Academic, London (2017)
33. Suchman, L.: Human-Machine Reconfigurations: Plans and Situated Actions, 2nd edn. Cambridge University Press, Cambridge (2007)

Concluding Remarks

This book has explored communication with generative AI as a distinctly human skill. Rather than treating AI interaction as a technical optimisation problem, it has framed it as a communicative practice shaped by intent, context, iteration, judgement and ethical responsibility.

Across the chapters, a consistent pattern has emerged. Misalignment in human–AI interaction rarely stems from technical failure alone. More often, it arises from unclear intent, insufficient context, implicit assumptions, misplaced trust or unexamined communication habits. Generative AI systems respond fluently to language, but fluency does not guarantee alignment. The burden of meaning-making remains fundamentally human.

By examining principles, techniques, common failures, collaborative practices and metacommunication, the book has argued for a shift in perspective. Effective AI interaction is not achieved by issuing better commands, but by cultivating communicative discipline. This includes learning how to frame tasks clearly, explore ideas without premature closure, manage constraints thoughtfully, structure dialogue iteratively and reflect on the interaction itself as it unfolds.

A central insight is that communication with AI is dynamic. Goals evolve, understanding deepens and interpretations shift over time. Treating interaction as a process rather than a transaction enables users to detect errors early, recalibrate expectations, and maintain cognitive alignment. In this process, AI output becomes feedback rather than authority, and dialogue becomes a shared space for reasoning rather than a one-way request–response exchange.

The book has also emphasised the ethical dimension of AI communication. Overtrust, undertrust and unreflective reliance on persuasive output can all distort human judgment. Responsible communication requires active evaluation, transparency about uncertainty, and awareness of how tone, framing and constraints shape AI behaviour. These are not technical safeguards alone; they are communicative responsibilities.

V. Geroimenko, *Communication Skills for Generative AI*, Human–Computer Interaction
Series, https://doi.org/10.1007/978-3-032-21689-2

Looking forward, the importance of AI communication skills will only increase. As generative systems become more multimodal, more persistent and more integrated into real-time environments, humans will need to communicate across text, images, documents, speech and other modalities with increasing fluency. Communication literacy will extend beyond writing prompts to managing relationships with adaptive, interpretive systems.

Yet the core message remains stable. No matter how advanced AI systems become, they do not replace human judgment, responsibility or meaning-making. They amplify human capacities, but they also amplify human communication habits—good and bad alike. The future of human–AI collaboration will therefore depend less on what AI can do and more on how humans choose to communicate with it.

This book does not propose a final model of AI communication. Instead, it offers a framework for reflective practice—one that readers can adapt as technologies evolve. If it encourages users to slow down, articulate intent more clearly, engage more thoughtfully and remain critically present in their interactions with AI, it will have achieved its purpose.

Communication with generative AI is not about surrendering agency. It is about exercising it—carefully, consciously and creatively.

GPSR Compliance
The European Union's (EU) General Product Safety Regulation (GPSR) is a set
of rules that requires consumer products to be safe and our obligations to
ensure this.

If you have any concerns about our products, you can contact us on

ProductSafety@springernature.com

In case Publisher is established outside the EU, the EU authorized
representative is:

Springer Nature Customer Service Center GmbH
Europaplatz 3
69115 Heidelberg, Germany